Kindling

Igniting a life of insight and purpose

WILLIAM CORWIN CLYDE

Kindling: Igniting a life of insight and purpose
Cottage Road Publishing
Second Edition

ISBN-13: 978-1492899518
ISBN-10:1492899518

Cover design by Vila Designs

Book design by Maureen Cutajar
www.gopublished.com

To our children

Contents

If–

By Rudyard Kipling

If you can keep your head when all about you
Are losing theirs and blaming it on you,
If you can trust yourself when all men doubt you,
But make allowance for their doubting too;
If you can wait and not be tired by waiting,
Or being lied about, don't deal in lies,
Or being hated, don't give way to hating,
And yet don't look too good, nor talk too wise:

If you can dream—and not make dreams your master;
If you can think—and not make thoughts your aim;
If you can meet with Triumph and Disaster
And treat those two impostors just the same;
If you can bear to hear the truth you've spoken
Twisted by knaves to make a trap for fools,
Or watch the things you gave your life to, broken,
And stoop and build 'em up with worn-out tools:

If you can make one heap of all your winnings
And risk it on one turn of pitch-and-toss,
And lose, and start again at your beginnings
And never breathe a word about your loss;
If you can force your heart and nerve and sinew
To serve your turn long after they are gone,
And so hold on when there is nothing in you
Except the Will which says to them: 'Hold on!'

If you can talk with crowds and keep your virtue,
Or walk with Kings—nor lose the common touch,
If neither foes nor loving friends can hurt you,
If all men count with you, but none too much;
If you can fill the unforgiving minute
With sixty seconds' worth of distance run,
Yours is the Earth and everything that's in it,
And—which is more—you'll be a Man, my son!

Preface

Before Tom Cruise, Matt Damon, Arnold Schwarzenegger, and even Clint Eastwood, there was John Wayne. The iconic action hero of my youth, "The Duke", as he was sometimes called, was famous for fighting, shooting, and tough-talking his way through every movie to protect the abused and vanquish the bad guys, wherever they were. To me, his characters seemed a source of stability on which I could build my sense of right and wrong. I loved going to movies to see the most recent John Wayne film, and believed that anything John Wayne did was, by definition, good. He was a role model to me.

And then an unsettling thing happened. There, in one of my favorite movies, The Duke was driving while clearly intoxicated. This was before MADD and SADD and national sensitivity to the dangers of drunk driving, but my awareness to the issue had been raised when someone very dear to me had almost been killed by a drunk driver. When that accident happened, I remember wondering why someone would risk lives—their own and others'—by driving a car when they could barely stand. It left a strong impression because I had almost lost someone close to me. It seemed irresponsible.

And, yet, here was my hero doing it in a movie. Two strong beliefs were in conflict: the infallibility of John Wayne vs. the insanity of driving drunk. This really troubled me and I couldn't stop thinking about it. Either I had over-reacted about drunk driving, and it wasn't really so bad (after all, there was no national uproar about it and everyone seemed to watch that part of the movie without comment) or John Wayne was not infallible. I felt strongly about both and was having a hard time letting go of either.

But this conflict opened my mind to a much broader issue: if this conflict was possible, it seemed likely that there were other things in my life that were not as sure as they seemed. I needed to consider and reconsider all things I believed to be true, continually comparing them and checking for inconsistencies and conflicts. And so began a life of perpetual questioning and reflection in search of consistent truths.

Luckily, I quickly found that others shared my struggle, and that many had written down their conflicts and conclusions—some were even in books my teachers were trying to make me read! The scientific method, the search for cause and meaning in history, the reflections of philosophers, the perceptions of poets—the resources available to me were as vast as any library. Nor were they confined to libraries: it seemed that everyone I met knew something from which I could learn—even if they didn't realize it. This is not to say that everything I read or heard was true— it all required thinking and sorting.

And now it is forty years later. Over this time I have found many things that seem to stand up to the rigors of reflection and that I believe to be true. Originally written for my children, this book is a distillation of what I believe I have sorted out. Like my kids, I believe that over time you will learn these things yourself, but you will have to distill them from writings that may be inconsistent or misleading. This book is meant to give you a head start (perhaps a forty year head start), both in thinking about and recognizing the specific ideas shared here as they manifest themselves in your life, but also in the way of thinking that will lead you to a life of intentionality and reflection—and discovery of many more such ideas. Sir Isaac Newton, who invented calculus and other mathematics as well as formulating many of the laws of physics, was fond of saying, "If I have seen further it is by standing on the shoulders of giants," thereby giving due credit to his predecessors in math and science. I offer this book so that you might stand on the shoulders of the giants I have discovered.

You will often hear the coach of a winning team talk about executing the "fundamentals" well—doing basic, known-to-be-important, things right every time. Most of the concepts in this book are "fundamentals," which I believe have broader impact and application than often understood. They are things I (and others) have benefitted by applying in a wide range of situations, whenever I have had the presence of mind to remember and apply them.

The ideas found here have been accumulated over many years, recorded on scraps of papers, on a mini recorder, and in voicemails, emails, and texts to myself (not while I was driving!) Aside from the advice in this book, I commend to you the practice of recording your ideas when they occur to you. This is common among all creative people, be they writers, scientists, musicians, or entrepreneurs. I once read an article about a singer/songwriter saying life is about "waiting for the bolts of lightning" and the rest of the time we are "just laying bricks." Each of the chapters represents a bolt of lightning that I hope will be as valuable to you as it has been to me.

In any book, the writer's world view is the foundation upon which all of the content rests. The perspective of this book is of one who has accepted the importance of faith and the role of God in life (though most of it is relevant and useful to someone who has not).

I share that perspective knowing that you will run into many learned people who believe that there is no place for faith—that faith and reason are not compatible. While not trying to debate the matter here, the most important thing I can convey is that it is simply not true that being a thinking person is incompatible with being a person of faith. Great thinkers past and present have wrestled with the compatibility of faith and reason and found essential roles for both in their lives. A list of some of my favorites is in the appendix (along with a list of other books I've found useful), and includes Tolstoy, Martin Luther King, Mother Teresa, and Francis Collins, the scientist who recently led the successful mapping of genes within human DNA. I hope you find them useful.

CHAPTER ONE

"Guard your character"

We have a video on Theodore Roosevelt which relates the advice his father gave him as he left for college. He didn't say, "Work hard." He didn't say, "Stay out of trouble." He didn't say, "Find your passion." He didn't say, "Consider this major or that," or, "Participate in this activity or that." He simply said, "Guard your character."

In some sense, that is what much of this book is about: valuing your character and living a life that exhibits the qualities you treasure most.

You must perpetually and intentionally choose that if your life is to reflect it. Challenges will come at you from all directions—including your own tendencies and desires—which will tempt you to compromise. That is not to say that flexibility is not important in relationships and life. But you must consciously consider whether that flexibility is simply letting go of the need to "have it your way," or whether it is compromising core values key to your character and identity. This can be most challenging when the conflict comes from within yourself: each of us has natural vulnerabilities—be they derived from genetics or environment—that test our capacity to do what we know is right. Managing those challenges builds our character. You may have heard a quote from the late Stephen Covey that captures the cost of such decisions:

> Sow a thought, reap an action
> Sow an action, reap a habit
> Sow a habit, reap a character,
> Sow a character, reap a destiny

Recent research increasingly tells us that character traits such as self-control, fairness, integrity, perseverance, zest, and gratitude may be as important as intellect in predicting success in school, career and life. Some schools have already begun including results of this research into their programming. With luck, these trends will continue. Whether or not they do, Theodore Roosevelt, Sr. gave his son very good advice.

CHAPTER TWO

Don't let your childhood get in the way

Throughout my life, it has amazed me how much self-impressions and identities seem to be formed by early relationships with parents, siblings, and others. I've had women tell me they feel pressure to be beautiful because of how often they were told they were beautiful as children. I've heard friends who grew up with dishonest adults say they have a hard time learning to trust anyone or anything. I've seen kids who were treated as favorites turn into adults who expect everything to revolve around them—and kids who grew up unable to get attention learning to find it by causing trouble, both as children and then as adults. I know so many people who have defined what they were good at not by how they did in the outside world, but by how they compared to siblings. Visit a nursing home, and you will be amazed to hear so many eighty- and ninety-year-olds tell stories about how their parents and siblings treated them at young ages—both good and bad—and to see the impact of that treatment in their self-perception, relationships, and lives.

No matter how hard your parents may have tried to encourage you to 'be your own person' and explore your own special talents and interests, you probably bear the prints of your understanding of your place in your family. Whether that understanding was right, wrong, or irrelevant, you most likely formed a large part of your identity within that context. Your challenge as you emerge as an adult is to keep that understanding, that identity, from confining you—to open your mind to how you relate and are perceived in the world outside your family and be able to transform your understanding of yourself to accommodate your fullest and most healthy identity.

There is a wonderful episode of VeggieTales, "A Snoodle's Tale" that helps make the point. It is a story of a child being physically given negative self-images (they are actually handed to him), which burdened him as he carries them around, preventing him from discovering his true potential. He eventually meets someone who removes these burdens, thereby allowing him to explore all he was born to be.

But self-images don't have to be negative to be confining and to keep you from perceiving who you can be. It is just as easy to feel responsible to live up to a positive self-image (which, don't get me wrong, can sometimes be good) as to feel burdened by a negative self-image. As Kipling says,

If you can meet with Triumph and Disaster
And treat those two impostors just the same;

Self-images are stories inside your head, which may not be consistent with reality—and may prevent you from exploring and achieving your potential.

You need to continually consider and guard against that. To the extent possible (I know this is hard), you need to hold these stories loosely—and let them go if they are harmful or limiting. Don't get type-cast by yourself or others. You don't need to be burdened by a history or reputation as a bully or a nerd or insensitive or a jock or a wallflower or whatever. You can and will change over your life—for the better if you work hard on it.

One way to see yourself anew is to consider how strangers see you. Remember that, "A prophet is honored everywhere except in his own hometown and among his relatives and his own family" Those who know you (including you) may have a hard time seeing change in you—may not be able to see who you are *now*. One of the great things about moving to a new school, a new job, or joining new groups is that people who don't know you will view you with "fresh eyes"—they are not blinded by stories they already have about you. Seek out new people and new experiences. They will help you grow—and help you see how you've changed.

CHAPTER THREE

Judging fish based on how well they climb trees

Finding your gifts can be so difficult. You may feel like you should be a good student, a good athlete, a good artist or a good musician because that is part of your family identity. Or you may avoid pursuing an area of development because a sibling is already good at it, or perhaps it is not valued in your family.

Albert Einstein said, "Everybody is a genius. But if you judge a fish by its ability to climb a tree, it will live its whole life believing that it is stupid." The challenge is not just to figure out if you are a fish or a squirrel or a bird, but what kind of fish you are. Are you fresh or saltwater? Warm or cold water? Bottom feeder or top feeder? Reading *7 Kinds of Smart* (on Multiple Intelligences, by Thomas Armstrong) will help you perceive a variety of gifts in yourself (while also helping you recognize and value those in others).

In the game of bridge, you assess the strength of the cards you are dealt, make a bid as to which suit represents your greatest strength and how many cards you will win playing with that suit as trump. The key to success in bridge is correctly assessing your strengths, both by correctly identifying their nature (what you are good at—the suit) and by accurately evaluating their extent, neither understating them (in which case you will bid too low and not achieve your potential) nor overestimating them [in which case you will bid too high and fall short of your goal (your bid) and lose.] It is hard to appreciate the value of this metaphor without knowing how to play, and I recommend learning to play the game, if only to appreciate the power of the metaphor (although you will learn many other things from the game).

The messages of Einstein's quote and the game of bridge are the same: Be content to discover and develop your gifts and yourself, instead of trying to be someone else or have gifts you really don't, which will simply lead to frustration and underachievement relative to your true gifts. That takes a lot of self-discipline and introspection—and candid counseling from true friends and mentors. It can be so easy to "lock in" on the first thing at which you excel, closing your mind to other things at which you might be even better—or to give up on something too soon, not realizing that the others you see doing it better have spent long hours of work to get so good. You need to be open to trying many different things, giving your all to each as you try them, and continually assessing your progress and proclivity.

Here is an important piece of advice relevant to exploration and development of all gifts: look for the right fit. People so often try to get themselves (or parents try to get their children) onto the most competitive team even though they may not be given the chance to play and grow and develop there, or into the most challenging class or school even though they may have trouble being successful and learning there. Others are content to be the star on a team or in a school that does not really challenge them or help them grow. Neither will help you understand all you can be. Neither will help you become all you can be.

Try lots of things. Give each your all while you are doing it. Seek the right level of challenge. Listen to good counsel. Seek to know yourself. And have fun!

CHAPTER FOUR

Shining your light without casting a shadow on others

Everyone wants to feel respected and valued. One of the most important things you can do in your life is to help people feel that way—and avoid making them feel small and unappreciated. Much of Dale Carnegie's good book, *How to Win Friends and Influence People* (a strange title for a book I believe is mostly about selflessness) deals with personal habits that will help you keep your ego in check and let you help others see their value and feel important. While I commend his advice to you for the pure purpose of helping others feel loved, you should know that, as Carnegie suggests, making others feel loved tends to make them feel love for you, trusting others tends to make them trust you, and making others feel important tends to make them think you are important. For these reasons and others, you will do well to honestly and authentically make others feel valued.

The challenge is that even your very presence can make others feel less important. Consider the children's story,

13

Hello, Great Big Bullfrog! by Colin West, in which the bull-frog feels smaller and smaller as larger and larger animals arrive. The larger animals do nothing but appear, but simply being there is diminishing to the bullfrog's spirit (more about his role in the next chapter). At the end of the story we learn that anyone can be in the larger role. You will find yourself in both the larger and the smaller role at different points in your life. The trick is to be able to handle each well.

It is also true that simply sharing your gifts can make people feel smaller and less important. This is a very hard line to walk, because I don't mean to suggest that you should not develop and apply—and enjoy—your areas of giftedness. You should simply be aware that whenever you get the highest grade on a test, score the most points in a game or create something of beauty, others may feel less accomplished, and so less important, as a result. This doesn't mean not to try. If people perceive you are pulling back for their sake, they will feel disrespected—and you will not be honoring the talents and gifts you have. The issue is more one of how and where you apply or demon-strate your gifts, and what you do with the power they give you. If you apply your gifts in ways that obviously contrast yours to those of others and demonstrates your superiority [telling your story with more accomplishments in response to them telling theirs with fewer, adding your better voice to theirs in song (as in the scene between the sisters on the cabin steps in "The Bodyguard"), joining a game you know you will dominate], that will make others feel small. You may remember Arnold Lobel's Frog and Toad story, *The Dream*, in which Toad is onstage with an announcer saying how great he is and Frog is in the audience shrinking with each announcement until he is gone.

If, on the other hand, you apply your gifts to serve others (assisting them in learning something, solving a problem, overcoming an obstacle or otherwise succeeding at something *they have identified*), that can make them feel successful, honored and important—so long as you are truly serving them and not "helping" with something you have decided they need.

It is vitally important to remember that you had nothing to do with your natural gifts, nor the setting into which you were born, and so neither should be a source of pride—feeling joy and giving praise that you are "fearfully and wonderfully made" is good, but pride relative to others is not. You need to discover what you are meant to do with your gifts—and your challenges. Think of your gifts as the hand you are dealt in a game of cards—you had nothing to do with its quality, so feeling pride in it makes no real sense. It is not the cards you are dealt, but how you play them—and playing a poor hand well can be as thrilling and as much an inspiration to others as playing a good hand well. But you will never be able to play any cards well if you are continually showing them off along the way. And, by the way, always keep playing until the hand is done (run through the finish line)—sometimes there are surprises, even when it seems that all is decided.

The good news is that, where people have great respect for you and your gifts, your power to build those people up is greater. In a sense, your gifts are like electricity, especially those you have in the extreme: If used humbly, carefully and lovingly, others will pick up a glow and become energized by them, but if you use them too forcefully or to show off, they will instead "shock" others and make them shrink from you. You may have heard of the book, *Zapp!*, by William Byham in which good managers "zapp" (energize and empower) employees, while poor managers "sapp" (drain and dispirit) them. It is as if you have some capacity that others recognize, and the greater your gifts, the greater the power to energize or shock.

One last tip: participating in things at which others are better than you will help balance the scales, giving them the chance to feel legitimately "bigger." This can open the path to relationships of mutual respect based on the gifts of each person. Relationships do not work very well when one party has all the respect and power. So let yourself—make yourself—play games you know you probably won't win. You might win something more important.

CHAPTER FIVE

Don't let the shadows of others discourage you

We spend so much of our lives comparing ourselves to others. Recent research on social media, for instance, links Facebook use with depression caused by thinking everyone else is having more fun and doing better than you are. Other research indicates that women feel less satisfied with their appearance after comparing themselves to pictures of other women (which they see constantly). It is well known that the holidays are filled with great sadness for many people specifically because they think everyone else is having a "real" Christmas.

This is, of course, nothing new. It's about envy and creating expectations based on what you see around you instead of what you see inside. It's about loving your neighbor as yourself from a different perspective. Instead of the usual focus on your neighbor, it's about you. You will have a hard time loving and accepting yourself if you are constantly comparing yourself to others. There will always be someone faster, smarter, stronger, better looking, more popular…. Don't get me wrong—friendly competition can be mutually beneficial. But unless you are able to celebrate the gifts and successes of others authentically and whole-heartedly, without considering their relation to your gifts and successes, you will have a hard time loving them and a hard time finding, developing, and celebrating your own gifts.

It does not matter who your father is. It does not matter who your mother is. It does not matter who your sister or brother is. It does not matter who your uncle, aunt, cousin, friend, whatever is. As hard as it may be, you need to get out of the shadows any of them cast—perhaps even physi-cally removing yourself for a time if necessary—to honestly understand and determinedly develop your own identity and gifts—and the responsibilities that come with them.

CHAPTER SIX

Don't cast a shadow on yourself either

Achieving your life's dream brings with it a curse: what do you do with the rest of your life that can possibly measure up? There are movies that explore potential consequences of success (*What Ever Happened to Baby Jane?* and *Eureka*, among others). There are articles on the challenges facing pro athletes upon retirement, once the childhood dream has run its course and they go from being sought after stars to being "regular" people: Divorce and bankruptcy rates soar in the first years of retirement as they struggle to discover who they are. A star among stars, Michael Jordan put it bluntly: "Now, when you get into the Hall of Fame, what else is there to do?" (Taken from *Michael Jordan: Life After Glory* by Mitch Albom.)

But the phenomenon is not restricted to pro athletes. Consider ex-presidents (Carter, Bush, Clinton, and Bush) who have exhausted term limits and can never again be "president of the United States". Neither is it restricted to the rich and famous. Consider someone achieving the dream of finishing high school...or college...or graduate school...or getting the big job. Or the woman who finally has the child of whom she always dreamt. Or parents dealing with empty nests. It is an issue for anyone setting a big goal and then achieving it: what comes next? And conclusive *failure* in a major project or goal can have a similar effect, leaving you without a plan and without the confidence to start again.

The answer to both challenges lies in your identity. It is easy to become so committed to the dream, the quest, the mission, that you have a hard time separating yourself from it—it becomes your identity. When it is over, whether through success or failure, it can seem like your reason for living is over. If the dream was attained, it is easy to make the rest of your life about "the good old days," living in the past, which eclipses your potential—and your responsibilities—in the present and future. If you failed to attain your dream it can seem like all is lost and you are incapable of any future success. You must seek to honor the past (both the successes and the failures), learn all you can from it, and commit yourself to making the most of whatever comes next. Otherwise, you will realize too late that you only lived a part of your life and missed many things that, while perhaps less thrilling than achievement of "the dream," may actually have been much more fulfilling.

The solution begins before the success or failure. It comes from not identifying the goal as you. It comes from not letting yourself expect that the goal—and the lifestyle associated with it—will always be there. It comes from remembering that you always were, are, and will be a "regular" person. It comes from continually remembering that neither you, nor your goal, is God.

CHAPTER SEVEN

Life is like a game of PIG

The card game, not the basketball game.

This is how it goes. Begin by picking out cards to make a "deck" that contains a four-of-a-kind for each player. Shuffle, and deal four cards to each player. Trying to accumulate four-of-a-kind, the dealer chooses one card from her hand and passes it to the player to her left. That player, in turn, chooses one card from his hand and passes it to the player at his left. Play continues until one player has accumulated four-of-a-kind, at which point she discretely sets her cards down and places her finger on her nose. Once one player has done this, the other players must notice and place their fingers on their noses and the last to do so gets a letter ("P" or "I" or "G"). The first player to accumulate the three letters of PIG loses the game. If you haven't played it for a while, play it a few times before reading on—it will make a difference in your understanding of what follows.

The game (also sometimes known as "Spoons") seems to be about getting four of a kind, but it is really about watching to see if someone else does. As each player eventually figures out, if you focus on getting four of a kind, you will lose.

Things in life are often not about what they seem to be. And figuring that out—and what they really are about—is crucial. People argue about one thing when they are really mad about another. You may go to activities that seem like they are about accomplishing one thing (like a ropes course, which might seem to be about learning to climb) which are really about something else (like building confidence or teams). Companies seem to be in one business (like professional baseball) when they are really in another business (like entertainment). You may go bowling on a date, but the goal is not to bowl your best, but to spend time together and learn about each other. This may seem obvious, but it is amazing how frequently we forget it. If you don't figure out and focus on what things are really about, you will miss their potential for making a difference.

Nowhere is this more true than in figuring out what your life is about. At first it seems like your life is about survival and building the best life you can by accumulating friends, knowledge, things, a family, etc. But you may find it is about more than all of those—and discovering that will unleash your potential for making a difference. Some stories of people who have realized that (and what they've done about it) are listed in the appendix–but I'm sure you can find (and create!) one on your own.

CHAPTER EIGHT

Finding your keys

You may have heard the story of the man discovered one night standing under a streetlight searching for his keys. When asked where he had lost them, he pointed to a place in the dark fifty feet away. When asked why he wasn't looking there, the man replied, "It's dark over there, and I can't see."

Such a strategy is obviously flawed, but it points to our tendency to focus—sometimes exclusively—on what we can observe instead of on what is important. We have a tendency to celebrate—and perhaps model off of—lives of people who are highly visible to us (movie stars, athletes, etc.), when there are others who may be better life models but are not as visible, their work showing up only in the shadows. Consider, for instance, Vasily Arkhipov. Serving on a crippled Soviet submarine off the coast of Florida during the Cuban Missile Crisis, he alone prevented his fellow officers from launching a nuclear torpedo on a nearby US aircraft carrier—an act that most agree would have touched off nuclear war. His courageous stand may have saved the world from total destruction, but no one knows his name. Ordinary people do extraordinary things every day, much of which goes unnoticed. But it still makes a difference.

When assessing the effectiveness of an action or process, we tend to focus on outcomes that are directly observable or have immediate impact. But often the true value lies in something that is not directly observable or not obviously important. In tennis or basketball it's easy to marvel at an explosive overhead smash or slam dunk, but fail to appreciate the preceding play that made those shots possible. In business economics it is much easier to focus on measurable revenues and costs experienced by the buyer and seller, rather than on harder-to-measure externalities—costs and benefits of the transaction experienced by parties apparently not participating in the transaction. These can be good, like when preserving a park enhances the value of homes in the surrounding area and the homeowners benefit without doing anything, or bad, like when products create pollution or waste, the cost of which is not borne by the producers or consumers. In either case, these externalities are important, but easily forgotten.

Our tendency to focus only on what we see can also challenge our faith. Let me share my own experience. Each person has some peculiar abilities. Somehow, I am able to touch someone's forehead and know his or her temperature within a half a degree. Somehow, I am also able to wake up in the night and know what time it is— usually within a few minutes and often exactly. Each of these is easily validated, but I don't understand either. Likewise, I can feel the presence of God in my life through a sensed purpose in apparently random events and interactions with others that defy logic in terms of timing and prescience. I am fully aware that things can happen by chance and that improbable things are often more probable than they seem. But that kind of thing happens to me ten or twenty times a day. At some point you have to think, "Something is going on here"—and you begin to see the hand of God in little things everywhere.

I have an inner sense this feeling is true in the same way as I know the temperature and the time. The only difference from those two is that it is not easily validated. So the question is the same as it is for the man looking for his keys under light: Does something being true require that we can observe or validate it? Does something being true require that there exists a logical argument to support it? I believe that it is important to try to subject all ideas to observation and analysis and not to accept unexamined dogma. But is it possible there are true things we will never be able to observe? Is it possible there are true things for which we will never find a logical argument?

I am a great lover of science, learning and knowledge. Yet it is far too easy, when we experience the exhilaration of discovery, to believe that we have, or can develop, complete understanding of things. It is so easy to become arrogant and make a god out of our knowledge or ourselves, forgetting there are still things we do not know and that there may be things—sometimes critical things—that will always be "in the dark." And that does not make them less true.

CHAPTER NINE

Chasing minnows

When I was young, my aunt and uncle lived near a lake in which we could swim and play. One of my favorite things to do was chase minnows with a small net about four inches across. My tendency at the beginning was to find a school of fish and chase the whole thing. As I did, the fluid, darting mass invariably avoided my net by successively splitting in two as I moved my net through the middle, hoping to catch a few. As each split occurred, I had to make a choice as to which half I would pursue. This would continue until I was chasing a single fish. It was not until that happened that I felt like I was finally chasing something definitive, and that if I relentlessly focused my attention and energy on it I might catch it (which I sometimes did). Before that focus on a single fish, I felt like I was chasing a cloud that kept vanishing in front of me.

I often thought of this experience later as I came to understand the tendency toward "chasing it all" in life. In general, you must determine your top priority and realize there may come times that other priorities will be sacrificed to achieving it. Rightly is it written, "No one can serve two masters". But we tend to have many, competing priorities and often want to take compromise measures that we hope will let us "catch lots of the minnows" at once. If we do that, we will almost always come to a time when the needs of the priorities split and a compromise measure will place us between the two splitting priorities—and we will come up empty.

CHAPTER TEN

Hardship is like getting a shot

You will experience hardship throughout your life.

It is tempting to think of hardship as either unfair, or a punishment for something you have done wrong. Clearly, many of life's hardships are the result of things we have said or done. Yet such hardships seem better characterized not as punishments, but as consequences that follow from our actions: if you throw a rock in the air it will fall down, perhaps on your head; if you yell at a friend, he may not seem very friendly for some time. If you pay attention, these will be learning experiences.

But sometimes hardship comes out of the blue and it seems clear you have done nothing to bring it upon yourself. Someone hits your legally parked car; it rains on a day that was supposed to be sunny, leaving you drenched; your boss is in a rotten mood, which he shares with you.... Seemingly random difficulties come into your life, sometimes hitting you all at once, and it can be very hard to take—and it seems unfair. As random and unfair as these may seem, I believe that they may be neither, and that they too can be for your good.

Consider a child getting a shot in the doctor's office. I can picture this scene with my own children so well. The one that stands out is the horror on my one-year-old daughter's face as the nurse came at her with the second needle in one visit. To my daughter, this experience was pure pain, with no understanding that there was a good reason for it. She looked at her mother and me to see whether we were really going to let this happen, and then, as if to ask whether this was really ok. Our looks of support, but sympathy, left her confused and perhaps a little mad, but ultimately bravely accepting—she trusted us enough to somehow know that the apparently senseless pain of the shot must be for her own good. And it was.

So too, it seems to me possible that hardship in life is there for good, even if we cannot perceive it at the time— and sometimes not even later. Hardship allows us to empathize. Hardship helps us remember the lessons experience teaches us. Hardship can expose necessity, which is the "mother of invention."

As adults, we often take hardship upon ourselves when we know we need it—giving up bad habits, diets, the "no pain, no gain" of exercise, and, yes, even shots.

Many other hardships seem senseless at the time, but, if we watch for it, we may come to understand their value. Such a situation is described by Corrie ten Boom in her book, *The Hiding Place*. Taken to a Nazi concentration camp for hiding Jews, Corrie and her sister, Betsy, have somehow smuggled a Bible into their barracks and are trying to run Bible studies and prayer sessions for their inmates, but fear reprisal by the always vigilant prison guards. One night during a prayer, Betsy suggests that they thank God for the lice covering their bodies. Corrie protests, but Betsy insists that they should thank God for all things, and so they pray, "God bless the lice." As time goes on, they recognize that the guards never seem to enter the barracks in the evening, leaving them free to worship. Eventually they discover that the guards are avoiding contact with the prisoners for fear of getting lice themselves, at which point they both pray with fervor, "God bless the lice!"

And then there are hardships that we will never understand, sometimes so atrocious that it is impossible to believe they can be good in any way—and we are left guessing as to the reason, if we are so motivated. Such was the situation in which Abraham Lincoln found himself toward the end of the Civil War when he wrote in a letter to newspaper editor Albert Hodges,

> I claim not to have controlled events, but confess plainly that events have controlled me. Now, at the end of three years struggle the nation's condition is not what either party, or any man devised, or expected. God alone can claim it. Whither it is tending seems plain. If God now wills the removal of a great wrong, and wills also that we of the North as well as you of the South, shall pay fairly for our complicity in that wrong, impartial history will find therein new cause to attest and revere the justice and goodness of God.

And then, in his second inaugural speech,

> Fondly do we hope, fervently do we pray, that this mighty scourge of war may speedily pass away. Yet, if God wills that it continue until all the wealth piled

by the bondsman's two hundred and fifty years of unrequited toil shall be sunk, and until every drop of blood drawn with the lash shall be paid by another drawn with the sword, as was said three thousand years ago, so still it must be said "the judgments of the Lord are true and righteous altogether.

We will never know all. Yet, if our faith is strong, as the "needle" approaches we can trust that this too is for good. With faith, we can see adversity as an opportunity to prepare ourselves for whatever comes next, or to see it as protecting us from something worse. And, with faith, we too can pray with all of our hearts, "God bless the lice."

CHAPTER ELEVEN

Life is full of Chaos

Most of us tend to assume that results change proportionally with inputs—that if we leave a little later we will get where we are going a little later, or if we study a little harder we will do a little better on the test. While that is often true, there are many situations in which it is not—situations in which a small difference at the beginning can result in a huge difference at the end. The study of such situations has developed into a new branch of science and mathematics over the past fifty years and is called Chaos Theory—aptly named for the havoc such "sensitive dependence on initial conditions" can create in your life. There is an amazing book that explains the development and uses of Chaos Theory, which I highly recommend: *Chaos: The Making of a New Science*, by James Gleick.

Some examples might help. I leave for work at five o'clock in the morning. I do this not because I am naturally an early riser, but because I know that if I leave then I will beat the traffic in which I will get caught if I wait and leave at six o'clock—if I leave at five o'clock I reliably get there by six thirty (one-and-a-half hours of travel), but if I leave at six o'clock I will not get there until eight o'clock (two hours of travel) and maybe not until nine o'clock (three hours of travel) if there is an accident, which is more likely with more traffic. If, on the other hand, I could wait until ten a.m. to leave, traffic would likely have dropped back off, and the trip would likely be back to an hour and a half. Sometimes the impact of small changes is even more extreme. Think of what happens if you miss a train or bus or plane by just a few minutes or even seconds. That small difference in your arrival time at the depot or gate will result in a large, and probably inconvenient, difference in how your day develops—you may end up not making the trip at all! The last five minutes of studying may lock the information in your brain in ways the first ten hours did not (you may finally "get it"), ensuring success on the test. This idea that small changes can beget disproportionally large changes is sometimes called the "butterfly effect," and is captured in an old nursery rhyme:

> For want of a nail, the shoe was lost,
> For want of the shoe, the horse was lost,
> For want of the horse, the rider was lost,
> For want of the rider, the message was lost.
> For want of the message, the battle was lost,
> For want of the battle, the kingdom was lost,
> And all for the want of a horseshoe nail!

Once you understand the idea, you will come to realize that we all experience the butterfly effect many times every day.

But there's more. It turns out that situations or systems that are sensitive to initial conditions can display very complex behavior—and there are many, many natural systems that display that sensitivity. Consider, for instance, weather, which was one of the first things to which Chaos theory was understood to apply. A very small change in temperature or pressure (even the beating of a butterfly's wings—thus the name, butterfly effect) can cause not just a large change in temperature or pressure, but a thunderstorm experienced a few weeks later: change in a chaotic system often happens not through a gradual, smooth process, but through turbulence. Thus it is expected that the most important short term manifestation of global warming (whatever its cause) is not the very slight increase in average temperatures around the world, but a very significant increase in the number of storms, hurricanes, and weather-related disasters—an increase in turbulence. This will likely have huge economic impact as property along coasts is repeatedly damaged, fruit crops are destroyed by late-winter temperature swings, and other consequences develop. We are already seeing that and should expect to see more.

The thing I love most about chaos theory is the way it helps us understand the complexity and beauty of the world. Simple chaotic equations can generate the endless variety of snowflakes, the placement of leaves on a tree (in fact, the shapes of the leaves themselves), the behavior of insects, and even "random" numbers—the "random" numbers generated by a computer are, in fact, not random, but generated by equations. Indeed, contemplating chaos theory makes me wonder whether anything in life is really random—perhaps everything is just an endless array of interacting chaotic systems, meaning, to quote Einstein, that "God doesn't play dice with the world." In any case, chaos theory makes me aware that everything I do may have more wide-ranging impact than I ever realized.

CHAPTER TWELVE

The difference between drowning and winning an Olympic medal

Consider two people in the middle of a pool: one drowning, one in the process of winning an Olympic medal. Each is trying hard, but one has a practiced strategy for moving by coordinating the motion of arms and legs, while the other is flailing desperately. Each is highly motivated, but one will be successful in achieving something wonderful and the other will fail in avoiding something terrible. Trying hard is not enough. You need to be trying in a planned and disciplined way if you are to be successful.

A person, a family, a business, a nation, and the world suffer from the impact of uncoordinated, undisciplined effort on a regular basis. Without a shared mission or goal, agreement as to how each member will contribute to that mission or goal, and preparation by each member to fulfill those roles, there will be a lot of "arm and leg" movement, but that movement will not be pushing in the same direction—and the efforts of various members will often offset each other.

It has been said, "if you fail to plan, you plan to fail." That is true for individuals and it is true for groups. It is the role of leaders to bring a group to agreement as to mission or goal, as well as agreement as to the way in which members will contribute to achievement of that goal. Each person has an inner sense of his or her potential and a desperate desire to fulfill it. I believe that it is the frustration of that desire that caused Thoreau to state, "the mass of men lead lives of quiet desperation." Great leaders find ways to allow people to unleash their potential, thereby fulfilling the deep desire of the members and creating a strong and motivated team.

An amazing story of personal planning and persistence is found in the life of Heinrich Schliemann. As a young boy, he became enchanted by the *Iliad*, Homer's account of the Trojan War. Despite the fact that others at the time believed it to be fiction, Schliemann dedicated his life to finding the lost city of Troy and proving it to be real. His plan included earning the fortune he would need for expeditions, learning languages so he could decipher texts, and becoming an expert in history, archeology, and other fields. In the end, he discovered Troy and other ancient cities, transforming both archeology and history. Not all plans will go so well as his, nor do they need to last a lifetime. But having a plan and executing it with determination will help you make the most of your gifts and your opportunities.

CHAPTER THIRTEEN

A seed won't grow into a flower in a day, no matter how hard you work

Teachers of small children often speak of certain skills being "developmental." By this they mean that the acquisition of that skill will develop in time with the aging of the child, and that premature practicing to try to "force" its development will likely only frustrate parent and child. We used to read our kids one of Arnold Lobel's Frog and Toad stories, *The Garden*, which made the same point in a very simple way: Toad planted seeds and kept yelling at them to grow, believing he could make them grow faster by his prompting. I've often thought that children's story is aimed more at the parents reading the story than the children hearing it.

The obvious, but easy to forget, fact is that some things will only happen through hard work and some things will only happen with the passage of time and some things take both. It is important to work hard and apply yourself to developing your gifts and making a difference in the world where you can. But it is equally important to humbly accept the nature of things where the passage of time is what's needed and any effort by you will be wasted energy, will frustrate you and may damage relationships.

The idea is crystallized in the Serenity Prayer by Reinhold Niebuhr:

God, grant me
The serenity to accept the things I cannot change,
Courage to change the things I can,
And wisdom to know the difference.

CHAPTER FOURTEEN

Don't give up!

It is easy to feel like you should be doing more or should have achieved something more important by now, but remember: Abraham Lincoln's life seemed full of failure until his final five years. He lost the Senate nomination of his party in 1855 and then lost the Senate election to Stephen Douglas in 1858. Yet he understood the importance of giving voice to his ideas and continued to do that, which eventually, to the surprise of most, resulted in the Republican nomination for president and the Presidency.

Failure has given several of history's great writers time and space—and sometimes motivation—to record their masterpieces. Among them, Marco Polo, John Bunyan, and Martin Luther King each wrote great works from prison. Winston Churchill was given time to record his invaluable first-person account of World War II only because he lost a stunning election in 1945. Einstein experienced his "miracle year," publishing four world-changing papers, having been rejected by academia and while working as an examiner in a patents office—and still did not get his first academic position until nearly three years later. Herman Melville died a forgotten man, with *Moby Dick* not being recognized as among the greatest works of American literature until long after his death.

In fact, many committed people, most of whom will never be famous, come to the end of their lives without understanding the impact they've had in the world. Your life's significance might not be obvious to you, but if you live with integrity and love, you will make a difference.

CHAPTER FIFTEEN

Seed corn vs. feed corn

If you travel the Great Plains, you will see vast fields of corn, soybeans, wheat, and other crops—mile upon mile for hundreds of miles of food for the nation and the world. If you are lucky, you will see a seed corn farm—the place where the product is grown not for consumption, but to seed the next crop for production. Sometimes seed farms are labeled as such, but you can recognize corn seed farms by the crops if you are there in August, after the tassels are out: corn crops meant for seed are grown by alternating varieties, several rows at a time, and the tassels of one variety are gone (people are paid to "de-tassel" them as the tassels are emerging) so that only pollen from the other variety will pollinate its seeds, thus ensuring cross-fertilization and the hybrid seed that is desired. The visual result is stripes of corn field alternating between stripes with tassels (which stand taller and more delicately topped) and those without tassels (which are shorter and more bluntly topped)—the latter producing the only seed that will be harvested as seed corn.

In olden times, seed corn was often just a portion of the crop that was set aside to ensure there would be seeds to plant in the coming year. As such, seed corn filled a sacred role—it was a sacrifice made as a bridge to the future. I am sure that there were many times when famished farmers were tempted to dig into the seed corn to stave off hunger at winter's end. But they resisted, understanding that they "would not reap where they did not sow" and that the grain for sowing was set apart from that for eating.

This same temptation is continually upon us even in the modern world, as our commitment to our future is constantly tested. The young adult must choose how much time and energy to commit to earning a living for today and how much to devote to the education that will open doors to opportunities for tomorrow. A philanthropist may have to choose between "giving a man a fish so he can eat for a day" and deciding to "teach a man to fish so he can eat for a lifetime." A nation must choose between spending resources on current consumption and investing them on the infrastructure that will fuel future productivity. The world must choose between using natural resources for food and building and jobs right now, and preserving the planet for posterity. None of these choices requires sacrificing all of one for the other. But each requires a sacred commitment of hope for our future. Each of us must make individual "seed corn" investment decisions for our own lives. Some of us are called to commit more—sometimes nearly all—of ourselves to the future, as parents, teachers, clerics, and other servants.

For most people, the choice is biased toward one direction—the here and now. Consumption of feed corn results in the immediate gratification of "Yum, this is good." Service as feed corn, on the other hand, takes patience and perseverance and faith as you must wait for the passage of winter before you can be planted, wait for the time it takes to germinate and grow, and trust in the timely arrival of sun and rain. I hope that you always have the patience, the self-discipline, and the courage to preserve and honor the seed corn within and among you.

I end with a related story. There once was a type of hand well pump that used a leather diaphragm to provide the suction that brought the water out of the well. One of these pumps was on a well in the middle of the desert, the only source of water for many miles. Infrequently used, the leather diaphragm would dry out and need to be wetted to soften it so that it could fulfill its role. Next to the pump was a bottle, which held just enough water to wet the leather so that a thirsty traveler could bring water out of the well. The ethical challenge was that amount of water in the bottle was also just enough to get a traveler to the next well. The question is, if you came upon the well knowing you would never pass that way again, would you risk emptying the bottle to wet the leather and preserve the resource for future travelers or would you drink it to ensure you would get to the next well, thereby imperiling those who came after you? It may seem an idle question, but it is not. And someday you will have to answer it.

CHAPTER SIXTEEN

A gift given in resentment is a burden, not a gift

I have often seen young children give birthday or Christmas gifts they wanted for themselves. The giver hovers over the receiver as he or she uses the gift, scoops it up as soon as it's set down, and dominates use of it for a time—sometimes, if the giver and receiver are siblings and therefore living in the same house, permanently.

This also happens with adults, but it is more common that the "gift" causing trouble is a sacrifice made on behalf of the other—which can cause much more trouble. I have seen this play out in families: there is disagreement about whether to try to have children, what color or which car to buy, where to live, how to spend holidays.... I have seen it play out in business setting: there is disagreement as to whom to hire, in which project to invest, what goal is being pursued, how best to pursue it.... It may seem a stretch, but I would say the same dynamic plays out with elections, in which a choice is made between people, parties, positions on a referendum.... In all cases, one party agrees or acquiesces to the other's wishes without truly giving in to the decision and grows to resent the arrangement as it develops.

Over time, the topic becomes a sore issue or flashpoint and lingers just below the surface, poisoning the relationship in a variety of ways that can seem unrelated. It becomes an instance of the game of "PIG."

The solution in all cases is the same: the giver must give the gift completely, letting go of his or her own desires, take joy in the joy of the receiver, and move on with life. (It is also important that the receiver not gloat at holding the prize, being sensitive to the sacrifice and struggle of the giver.)

But truly giving up the gift can be so difficult. The child may have chosen to give something she herself dreams of owning, but fears she never will. The adult may have understood the logic or necessity of giving in, but has not emotionally let go of having it his way—and may still believe his way is better. The people may earnestly feel that the election result puts critical principles in jeopardy. But there will be other gifts, other decisions, and other elections. And if we can only live in harmony when we receive the gifts, make the decisions, and win the elections, we will never live in harmony, since there must always be those on the other side of each transaction. We must learn to give the gift fully, submit to the decision completely, and accept the loss graciously, seeking to build relationships and community through our sacrifice.

CHAPTER SEVENTEEN

Helping vs. Serving

This may seem a fine line, but let me draw the distinction which I have seen made and strikes me as valuable. *Helping* is when I believe I have something you need and seek to give it to you. The implication is that I know what you need and am giving it to you, placing me in a position of superiority. There is a sense that my motivation may be my own feeling of self-satisfaction. Evidence that I am "helping" may come in individual choices in the action which prioritize my needs instead of yours. If you sense that is my motive, my help will be alienating, and you may reject it.

Serving, on the other hand, is when I place myself at your disposal. Serving means I am willing to do what you decide you need. Serving can mean giving you means to meet your own needs—or removing impediments that keep you from doing that. It is about teaching you to fish for yourself instead of just giving you fish. It may mean sharing some information that might better inform your understanding of what you need, but that is a slippery slope into "helping" and must be handled with respect. When I am "serving," individual choices within the action will prioritize your needs instead of mine.

Remember that no one else can give you happiness—in fact, they can take it away by trying to do too much for you.

My family's visits to the nursing homes have been an attempt to serve the people there. We never know what will happen when we are there. Sometimes someone we usually visit is gone for the day or asleep. Sometimes someone needs us to move them or put on a bib or get something. Sometimes someone who usually wants to talk does not want to talk at all—and sometimes someone who will never talk wants to dominate the conversation. While there, we always try to "play it by ear," seeking to sense the needs of the patients and do what they want.

In fact, our visits began with such a sensing: my wife and I were originally going to visit my grandmother, but it quickly became apparent that all of the patients seemed to enjoy our—and particularly, our children's—presence. We realized this was a service in which the entire family could participate—that, far from being a burden, our kids were actually the "stars of the show." Although we have sought to keep the focus of these visits on the needs of the patients, this service has been a blessing to our whole family: we have heard first-hand accounts of life during the Great Depression and throughout the twentieth century, seen inspiring character in the face of hardship, and developed friendships with people of vast life experience—all while giving each of our children the chance to interact with adults who really wanted to talk with them.

CHAPTER EIGHTEEN

Accepting vs. Enabling

This is a very hard one—but critically important if you are to play a positive role (or even just avoid playing a negative role) in the lives of others. *Accepting* someone means you love him or her unconditionally and will do so no matter what he or she does to you, himself, or anyone else. *Enabling* means making accommodations for, or even accepting blame for, the destructive behavior of others. The former allows the accepted person to work through challenges and grow without concern for losing important relationships, while the latter allows the enabled person to persist in behavior that is harmful to him/herself and/or others without feeling pressure to change. This distinction is important to understand in all relationships, be they friendships, work related, or family. Nowhere is it more critical than if you are a parent, where, by the very nature of the relationship, you are responsible to help your child grow.

The key thing is that loving someone *does* mean you love them no matter what, *but does not* mean you should protect them from the consequences of their actions (within bounds, of course—a child crossing the street may not live long enough to benefit from lessons learned from the consequences of not looking both ways; in such cases, "substitute" consequences are a good idea). If your toddler likes to climb and you catch her every time she falls, she will learn that she can climb higher and higher and fall without cost, which will be very dangerous for her the first time you are not there; better to let her fall early from small climbs so she comes to understand the risk involved. If your child forgets to do his homework, doing it for him will only prevent him from suffering the consequences of his omission—consequences which would, over time, teach him to be more responsible.

Failing to allow children to learn from consequences at an early age can easily lead to more dangerous enabling behavior later. Accepting someone who is chronically late can mean understanding when they "miss the bus," while always making everyone else wait for them can be enabling. Accepting a person who struggles with alcoholism means supporting their efforts to deal with it, forgiving them when they fail, and lovingly confronting them when they persist. It does not mean giving them money you know they may use to buy a drink, making excuses for them or allowing destructive behavior to continue unchecked. Accepting a person who displays abusive behavior means confronting the behavior when it appears, helping the person find help in overcoming the behavior, and loving the person through it all—even when you are the abused. It does not mean taking responsibility for their abuse because you did something to provoke it (even if you did do something, that is a separate issue and does not excuse escalation to abuse), or unnecessarily subjecting yourself to continued abuse. A true friend will always accept, but never enable.

This is a great challenge at the societal level. We wish to accept and love the pregnant un-wed teenager, but want to avoid enabling or promoting that state. We want to help those in need and teach them to help themselves to the extent possible, but want to avoid sapping them of the need and will to be self-sufficient. Creating safety nets to protect people from catastrophe makes sense, but we must ensure that those safety nets, meant to catch people if they fall, do not turn into trampolines, on which people plan to continually land.

CHAPTER NINETEEN

Misusing hammers

You should know that any group you will be a part of in life will have members who say or do things which you feel don't represent the group. I can tell you from personal experience that it is sickening and disheartening to see a cause or vocation to which you are devoted slandered and compromised by some who are thought to represent it. I'm talking about abuse committed by priests and teachers, cops who are "on the take," and soldiers who commit atrocities when the majority of people in those professions are dedicated to building trust, community, and peace.

It's vital to know that the presence of such members does not reflect on the virtue of the entire group—though opponents may hold those members up as evidence that the group as a whole is unworthy of respect or even existence. Remember that anything can be used for ill.

Consider a hammer. Used as intended, it can be of great use and improve our lives. But that doesn't mean it can't be used for evil if someone decides to do that. You would not be dissuaded of the value of hammers because someone used one to commit murder. Or even if some gang started using it as a weapon of choice. You need to know you don't have to defend such abuses or abusers.

A powerful example of this is in the use of religion generally, and Christianity specifically. Most religions focus on the inner life of the believer, providing pathways to tranquility in an often unsettling world. And yet, the peace they promise can easily be perverted by those seeking power. With few exceptions, adoption of religion by the government is a key indicator that such perversion may be going on.

Christians, for instance, persisted through often ghastly persecution for three centuries, during which the number of believers grew rapidly, despite the costs and dangers. But the first act of a government adopting Christianity as a state religion was the appearance of Chi and Rho on the shields of Constantine's troops as he led them into battle outside of Rome. Notwithstanding the accounts of Constantine's visions that led him to believe this act was the will of God, it seems absolutely antithetical to Christ's teaching to "love your enemy." It also seems at odds with Christ's direction to "render unto Caesar what is Caesar's and render unto God what is God's," indicating separation of church and state in the life of the believer. It does, however, seem consistent with the story line of "Meet John Doe," the Frank Capra film about a popular political movement being co-opted by someone seeking to harness its power for his own purposes.

Since this first adoption as the state religion, many have sought to use Christianity to justify their actions. People have been tortured and wars fought in the name of Christianity, including the Crusades, during which Christians were incited to the slaughter of Jews, Muslims and even other Christians *by church leaders.* The atrocities committed as "the will of God" over the centuries have been—really, there is no word for them. No wonder Gandhi was quoted as saying, "I like their Christ, I don't like their Christians," and Nietzsche wrote, "I will believe in the Redeemer when the Christian looks a little more redeemed."

The central elements of Christianity are,

- Love and serve God
- Love all people—including yourself and your ene-mies—as if they were God
- Serve all people as if they were God
- Forgive all people (including yourself) all things.

These basic elements are pervasive in Christian teaching. As such, anyone—be it Constantine, church leaders, popes, or presidents–representing Christianity in ways at odds with any of them is misusing a very important and powerful hammer.

One more thing to remember: such abuses of things you love will be all too obvious to you, but it is easy to miss such abuses of groups or causes with which you are not affiliated, to which you are not drawn, and with which you may even disagree. Try always to assume positive intent, do your research before taking a position, and try to see things from the other person's perspective.

CHAPTER TWENTY

You can lead a horse to water, but if you feed it salty pretzels...

When I first became a teacher, I had a very naïve understanding of the learning process. I am embarrassed to say that I literally spoke of trying to "download" my knowledge to my students. With that not going very well, I remember sitting in my office at the end of one day and commiserating with another first-year teacher who, in exasperation exclaimed, "I'm teaching them so much but they're not learning anything!" I recognized immediately that this was an almost comical admission that we had a problem.

As I drove home, the old saying, "You can lead a horse to water..." kept coming to mind. I was trying to lead my students to knowledge and understanding, but they seemed to have no interest in it. I wondered about my choice to leave banking, at which I had felt I was pretty good, to teach, at which I seemed pretty bad. Committed to the choice, I realized I could not live my next thirty years with the frustration of indifferent students. And then it occurred to me: if I somehow fed the horse salty pretzels, it would ask me—perhaps even desperately—where the water was, and gulp it down once found. My job was not to deliver water, but to create thirst. (This is another example of "Life being like a game of PIG"—things not being what they appear.)

With that revelation, my focus changed. As preparation, I needed to know that the necessary information was available, plan out the sequencing of learning wherever concepts built on each other, and define the scope of material it was reasonable and expected we could cover in a term. But my focus was to construct experiences and activities that would create thirst. My job was to motivate them to learn—and even to learn to learn. Teaching was about me, while learning was about them. This needed to be about them.

A great example of that changed focus in action came in an international finance course filled with foreign exchange calculations. My original strategy had been to demonstrate each calculation, answer questions, give homework, review homework in class, and give tests. My new strategy was to expose my students to the excitement of the trading environment by having them "play with" (do labs in) a foreign exchange market simulator in which they would need to know the calculations to be successful. I designed labs in which students explored features of the market, progressing to higher levels of complexity and calculation as they built understanding. Instead of me having to nag them to practice calculations, students now yelled at each other for messing up calculations in the heat of trading (they worked in two-person teams) and learned from each other. Instead of looking at their watches and beginning to slam books closed five minutes before class ended (as signals to me that they were ready to leave), they would be so engrossed in trading that I had to remind them it was time to leave and practically push them out the door so the next class could get in—with them talking excitedly about the concepts as they left.

While I think of this idea in terms of teaching, it's relevant to any situation in which you are leading. As I discuss in the chapter on Leadership, I see the role of leaders more as crystalizing consensus and sharing the vision—thereby empowering, energizing and focusing the team—than as telling people what to do. Motivated people, like motivated students, will bring all of their energy and gifts to what they do, creating a powerful team.

Not all situations lend themselves to such strategies, but motivating learning and other work wherever possible provides credibility and energy that can bridge the gap where such strategies are not possible and "we just need to get this done."

CHAPTER TWENTY-ONE

Life lessons on pricing and markets

When my oldest son was four or five years old, he set his mind on raising twenty-five dollars to buy something he had seen in a store. For some reason, he decided he was going to make that amount by selling rocks he found in the yard. Though the rocks were hand-picked and washed, this seemed a tough thing to accomplish, both because rocks are everywhere in Connecticut (supply was plentiful), and because he set up his "store" on the back porch of our house at the end of a cul-de-sac backing up to acres of woods – not exactly a high traffic area. At first, he priced the rocks at twenty-five cents each, reasoning that to be a fair price and hoping he could sell one hundred of them to attain his twenty-five dollars. But after a few weeks with no sales, he decided to change the price of each rock to twenty-five dollars, hoping to make his target with a single sale. Shortly after the price change, the dean of the school of business in which I worked came to dinner and observed the display. His area of expertise was marketing and he was greatly entertained by my son's pricing strategy being based, as it was, so clearly on his revenue needs instead of any relationship to market value.

I have thought of this story often when seeing similar pricing decisions from intelligent adults in a variety of markets. Back when I was trading currencies, it was not uncommon to hear someone in a losing position say he was going to hold it until it returned to the price at which he had bought it. No consideration for the fact that it might go a very long ways in the other direction (exposing him to a much worse losing position) before it returned to his level—or that if and when it did return to his desired level, market forces might carry it significantly higher so that selling at that point would be the wrong thing to do. The trading decision was based on the price needed to get back to even. Such pricing is even more prevalent with housing, where homeowners have little market pricing expertise and often ignore the advice of realtors. Ask any realtor and he or she will tell you that sellers often stubbornly price the house based on what they've put into it (original purchase price plus any improvements) or the peak value they believe it ever reached, instead of any reasonable estimate of current market value.

The answer to all of these is to honestly and objectively assess reality and base your pricing decisions on "what is" instead of "what you wish were true." Only by understanding and accepting the world as it is will you fashion strategies that are rational and potentially successful.

CHAPTER TWENTY-TWO

You are a role model

George Orwell's classic futuristic novel, *1984* (hard to believe that 1984 was futuristic at some point, isn't it?), warns of a world in which everyone is being watched by Big Brother—an all-powerful government with the ability to see and record everything anyone does through a vast network of electronic eyes. Many worry these days that, between all of our security cameras, webcams, vast databases used for anything from national security to marketing, the development of biometrics, and even implanted identity chips, we are moving eerily close to Orwell's vision.

But I want to tell you that part of that vision is already—has always been—true. You *are* being watched: not by Big Brother, but by little brother and little sister, by nieces and nephews and classmates and coworkers; by people you know well, by people you hardly know, and, thanks to the Internet, by people you will never know. What they see *is* recorded—in their memories and in the influence you have on their behavior. And it contributes irreversibly to the evolution of our culture, our species, and our world.

No matter who you are, you are being watched all of the time. Whether you realize it or not,

- the way you speak to people,
- your willingness to go the extra mile to get the job done—and done right,
- how you use your time, money and other resources,
- the extent to which you are reliable and accountable—

all of these and much more are observed by those around you—and may be imitated by them.

In no place will this be more true than if you are lucky enough to be a parent. The extent to which your kids will model off of you is shocking, sometimes gratifying, and often embarrassing—you see things you do in a different way when your kids start doing them.

- The way you deal with your mistakes
- The way you deal with the mistakes of others
- The way you deal with success
- Your commitment to service
- Your love of learning
- Your relationships with others
- Your relationship with God

All of these and so much more will be reflected in the eyes, and ultimately in the character of your children.

And it's not just your kids watching. As I've said, it's other people's kids, friends, co-workers, people who know you well, and people who don't know you at all. I'm not saying every single action is being watched, but every action may be, and you don't get to decide which is. There are countless less positive examples I could offer, but consider Rosa Parks and her decision to stay seated when ordered to stand. Did you know that three other African-American riders followed the order that day and stood, leaving her alone as a model to inspire a movement and a nation?

And the impact of your modeling can become infinitely deeper and broader than the people watching you, as those people share their own versions of your modeling with others, who share it with others—did you know that research shows that happiness can spread up to three degrees (from the originator to her set of friends, to their sets of friends, to their sets of friends) in a social network (including online social networks), and that obesity, sadness, smoking, and other behaviors are "contagious"? The power of your modeling is truly awesome—it may be your greatest legacy, no matter what else you accomplish in life.

A key part of being a good role model is choosing good role models for yourself. As children, we may not think much about our role models, blindly following those presented to us. But as adults, we have the opportunity—and the responsibility—to choose our role models carefully—to choose those who will challenge us to lead noble lives. It can be so easy to be drawn into admiring—and then unconsciously modeling yourself upon—someone who is exciting, rich, beautiful, brilliant, whatever, without really considering whether their character, priorities, and life are things you want to mimic. If you are a husband and truly wish to love your wife, search for someone you think does that really well and observe him closely—or even ask to be mentored by him. If you are a wife earnestly desiring to respect your husband, observe someone you think does that really well and ask for her guidance. If you are a parent seeking to challenge and nurture your children, find a family whose children you admire, and ask their parents

61

for their secrets. Whether as a student, an employee, a friend, spouse, or a parent—in any role you ever find yourself—you must be very intentional about those you honor as role models if you are, yourself, to be a worthy role model.

Finally, the challenge to you—to us—is this: to live every day, to strive that every word, every motive, every action, seen or unseen is something you would be proud to see others learn from you. Because learn from you they will.

CHAPTER TWENTY-THREE

Don't be tricked into singing along with lyrics just because the melody is good

It's hard to understand the emotional effect of music—how soothing, relaxing, uplifting, terrifying, or electrifying a good tune can be. It is scary, however, how easy it is to sing along with virtually any lyrics if the tune is stuck in your head. I always try to understand song lyrics, get their message, and think about why the author wrote them—and often I conclude that the message and motive are inconsistent with my beliefs and perhaps dangerous. And yet, I regularly catch myself humming or playing the tune of such a song in my head, with the lyrics floating along either in my brain or on my lips.

While music's effect may be singular, other things can have similar effects: something or someone of great beauty, an eloquent essay or speaker, a good story or movie, and even a friend. Anything that causes you to let your guard down can have this power. You must be aware of it all of the time.

Let me explain why I think it is dangerous to just "sing along" without thinking about the meaning of things. The first problem is that when I sing along, somehow, I believe those lyrics then become part of my thinking. Somehow, the lyrics become a sort of Trojan horse, sneaking words and ideas I would never say into my vocabulary and brain, possibly to reappear in my words and actions without my even realizing it.

The second problem is that people may be watching and modeling off of me at any time. To the extent some-one else *has* thought about the lyrics and respects me enough to value my opinion, hearing me sing along will make them think I think the lyrics are acceptable and per-haps lead them to decide they are acceptable too. Thus someone vulnerable to me as a role model may be led astray by my mindless acceptance.

The third problem is related to the first two, but more broadly stated: that we live in a time of transition (which can probably always be said), and there are always people with agendas seeking to influence that transition. Some of those will be willing to use subtlety to encourage others to follow a path they would not follow if they were thinking. Websites, TV, movies, books, newspapers, and other media may seem innocuous, but subtly send strategic messages to influence us and get us to go along. The Holocaust is an extreme example of what happens when people mindlessly "sing along" until it is too late—it's going on all the time with a wide range of consequences.

I say this not to scare you, nor to ruin your enjoyment of music or anything else, but to help you realize you must be thinking all of the time, and be careful about the lyrics you sing.

One last note: There is, of course, a positive side to all of this. That is a powerful reason to memorize favorite verses, poems, speeches, and sayings—to have their challenges, inspiration and insight floating around in your head wherever you go. I cannot tell you how often, for instance, the wisdom of the poem at the beginning of this book has come to mind, comforting and testing me as I encounter life's opportunities and dangers. Memorizing great words will serve you well—you may even find yourself quoting them!

CHAPTER TWENTY-FOUR

Leadership

Philosophers and researchers have long sought to understand the attributes, motives, and situations that result in leaders who will best serve their organizations or people. Plato referred to the "true ruler" as one who "doesn't by nature seek his own advantage but that of his subjects." Implied in this statement is the idea that, broadly speaking, there are two types of leaders: those who seek power for its own sake, and those "true rulers" who do not desire it, but accept it for the common good. Much can be said of the causes and costs of the former, which is all too common, but I focus on the latter here.

The concept of the Servant Leader draws on ancient foundations in Indian, Chinese, Christian, and other traditions going back 2500 years, yet seems to capture a modern ideal. Servant leaders are,

- **Community Builders**, evidenced by successfully reaching out to others (including others of unlike minds), consensus building, and being able to empower and inspire others to believe in themselves and the group,

- **Convinced of the Value of People**, truly modeling respect for all people, including those with whom they disagree or share little in common,
- **Good Listeners**, recognizing underlying and unspoken concerns of others and including them in subsequent discussion and problem solving,
- **People of Foresight and Vision**, perceiving the possibilities, implications, and consequences of actions and ideas in ways that are unusual and add value, and articulating a vision that seems both realistic and desirable,
- **Good and Determined Problem Solvers,** discovering creative solutions where there seem to be none, and persevering when others have tired, and
- **Good Educators**, being able to explain complex issues so that they are better understood, apply logic that adds insight but is understandable, and ultimately, persuade by convincing.

I recommend you work to develop these qualities in yourself to the extent you are able, as they will serve you well, whether you are a leader or a follower.

In any case, you must be ever vigilant to support good leadership around you, and be willing to provide leadership where there is none, even when you do not desire such a role. The cost of poor leadership is greater than most imagine and it is all too common when people become complacent. Left unchecked, those who desire leadership for its own sake will assume leadership, and their decisions will prioritize what is needed for them to retain power instead of what is in the best interest of those they lead.

CHAPTER TWENTY-FIVE

America's Greatest

A former student of mine was buried yesterday. He had been serving in Iraq, and was killed when a car bomb exploded as he investigated a parked vehicle.

He was such a good guy. In class, he was friendly, funny, and never afraid to ask questions—not a common attribute among students. Clearly, he had been in situations worse than my classes. By the time I met him, he already had significant military experience, which was evident in the way he carried himself, the way he spoke—even in his sense of humor. Whenever he thought I was pressing the class too hard he would chime out, "Thank you sir may I have another"—a comparison, I assumed, to a drill sergeant who was pushing too hard. He added life wherever he was. He was 6'4", built like GI Joe, proud to be an American and to serve, but not prideful. He was personable, outgoing, and fun. He was exactly who we wanted to send to represent us in a foreign country, but someone it's hard to imagine we have to do without.

In the words of his best friend, he was motivated to be there to secure the area and deliver food. His last act confirmed that his mentality was that of a protector—as he realized the car was a bomb, he pushed a fellow soldier out of the way. That soldier is alive today thanks to that sacrifice. As is true of so many other Americans lost in combat, his service and life were the greatest and most generous gifts we could share with the world.

It is hard not to ask yourself whether his sacrifice—and that of so many others—was necessary. The matter is muddied by the fact that our presence in Iraq was complicated by mixed motives. But there are other places and situations that make less complicated calls for help: Sudan…Congo…Burma…human trafficking….

What, if anything, is our obligation in such circumstances? This is where idealism and reality meet. When I have discussed it with my kids, we have done it in more local terms. If you know someone is being bullied, should you intervene? What if you know or can see someone is being seriously hurt or might be killed? What if intervening includes the likely cost of you getting hurt? If we as a family knew someone was being abused in a house down the street should we intervene? Would we feel or be responsible if something terrible happened and we did not?

What if, in the extreme, we knew abuse was going on right now and that someone might very well die unless we personally intervened immediately? Would we be responsible to? Could we afford to? If I left our house to intervene and were killed in the process would my family think it was worth it? Would it make a difference if we believed the abuser was also an immediate threat to our family? Getting back to the global view, should we have intervened earlier to stop the genocide in WWII? How is that different or the same as stopping what has been going on in the Sudan? Are our responsibilities different? Do we have any responsibilities? Do we need a self-defense component to warrant intervention? Is it the world's right but not responsibility to intervene in such cases? Or is it a responsibility whether or not there is a self-defense component and despite the cost?

Whatever the answers to these questions, for now, we are left with some of our best citizens representing us and dying in Iraq and around the world. New York calls its police "New York's Finest" and its firefighters "New York's Bravest." We should have a name like that for those serving us in the military.* My sense is that, like my former student, the vast majority are peacekeepers in their hearts, protecting people who are not yet ready to protect themselves from ruthless bullies who would very willingly—almost happily—dominate, torture, and kill them. "*Greater* love hath no man than to lay down his life for another." "America's Greatest." That seems to fit my former student well.

---

* And their families. It is hard—impossible really—for me to imagine how the families of service men and women cope with the separation. Knowing that mom or dad will be gone for what seems like forever—and that there is some possibility (s)he won't return at all... The uncertainty must wreak havoc. We often talk about the sacrifices made by service men and women, but the sacrifices of their families seem as great.

CHAPTER TWENTY-SIX

Cycles

I once saw a movie in which someone was trying to get a large statue into his second floor apartment. He had rigged up a rope and pulley from the roof of the building and someone on the roof was pulling the statue up to the second floor so that the owner could pull the statue in through a large window. The problem was that the statue was hanging too far from the building for the owner to pull it in—he could touch it, but could not get hold of it. He resolved the problem by pushing the statue away hard enough that it came into the room on the rebound. I've thought of that often with people and situations. Some things need to get worse before they can get better and you need to accept that.

People dealing with personal difficulty or in the midst of conflict, for instance, sometimes need to go away from community or the difficult situation before they can return in peace and find reconciliation. I know that each person must struggle with faith and go through periods of doubt if faith is to be his or her own. In each case you need to have the wisdom, patience, and faith to let people go—chasing them down may only delay or even prevent the eventual return.

More broadly, what I am talking about is cyclicality, which is everywhere, but not always perceived. Cyclicality may, for instance, tend to appear across time in families. There is an old saying, present in many cultures and languages, that captures this tendency, the American version being, "There are three generations from shirtsleeves to shirtsleeves." The idea is that the first generation makes sacrifices working long hours at low paying jobs to give the second generation the education and other advantages necessary for "a better life." The second generation is inspired and driven by the sacrifices of the first and achieves that dream, but raises a third generation which has not witnessed the sacrifices, takes the "living the dream" for granted, has trouble finding purpose, and does not cultivate the qualities necessary for continued success. It is interesting that John Adams recognized this cycle as an evolution, writing to his wife, Abigail, in 1780:

> I must study politics and war that my sons may have liberty to study mathematics and philosophy. My sons ought to study mathematics and philosophy, geography, natural history, naval architecture, navigation, commerce, and agriculture, in order to give their children a right to study painting, poetry, music, architecture, statuary, tapestry, and porcelain.

The question is whether a generation studying only "painting, poetry, music, architecture, statuary, tapestry, and porcelain" can perpetuate the resources required to sustain those studies in future generations.

An alternative generational model has been proposed

by researchers William Strauss and Neil Howe, who suggest that there are, in fact, four generations in a nation-wide cycle, each with its own characteristics (Millennials and Baby Boomers are recent manifestations of generations they propose), the successive appearances of which they trace back almost 700 years. Their model is more truly cyclical in the sense that the behavior of each generation fosters the behavior of the next, whereas the "shirtsleeve to shirtsleeve" model ends after the third generation with no promise or expectation it will regenerate.

In a larger context, there will inevitably be swings in politics, economics, and culture of a society. Voters may swing toward one party or ideology, but will eventually turn toward another as the value of the first has been delivered, its ideas spent, and the value of the second is desired or needed. Economies slow when producers and/or consumers develop too much inventory, and can only begin to recover when inventories are reduced, causing consumers to consume again and producers to produce again, thereby creating jobs.

And, on a longer timeline, history shows us that civilizations go through cycles of conquest, consolidation, civilization, and, eventually, decline—opening the possibility of conquest by another civilization. These historical cycles can be seen to parallel the shirtsleeve to shirtsleeve cycle in that investment in infrastructure, education,—the future—made in early stages fuel the success, but are no longer made at levels that will sustain that success in latter stages of the cycle (think of my question in response the John Adams' quote above). Also like the shirtsleeve to shirtsleeve cycle, there is no promise or expectation that the former glory of the civilization will regenerate: toward the end of the cycle trade suffers, economies contract, and the capacity to make the required investment in infrastructure and human capital without significant sacrifice—the kind that created the potential for success in the first place—is reduced beyond recovery.

Really, I am just telling you something you know, but need to remember when it presents itself: some things are cyclical. Some cycles are beyond your control and simply need to be accepted (like those related to the rotation of the earth) and some you can influence through planning, discipline, perseverance, and resilience (some of the important character traits discussed in the first chapter of this book), but cyclicality seems to be embedded both in the physical world, and in human nature. Remembering that can give you some of the wisdom you seek in the Serenity Prayer.

CHAPTER TWENTY-SEVEN

Balance is critical

A sports rivalry is not a rivalry if the same team wins every time. Based on history, one nation is more likely to become the aggressor and start a war if it believes it has greater power.

One of the tensions in life is that people naturally seek to draw power to themselves, yet the concentration of power is generally not healthy for anyone. Healthy relationships are built on parties having mutual respect for each other and each having some sense of self-worth and self-determination But that is difficult if power is concentrated in one of the parties. At a personal level, husbands and wives, siblings, and friends all need to feel valued and respected by each other if they are to be open to real and enriching relationships. This is related to the earlier discussions about not casting shadows on others and not being discouraged by the shadows of others. There is much literature based on the stress that flows from unbalanced relationships, among them, *A Separate Peace.*

Balance is also critical at the intra-personal level—in fact all balance probably starts there. You may have heard the expression, "Moderation in all things—including moderation." School, career, volunteering, friends, family, and self each deserve your attention, but each may demand more than is appropriate, putting the attention deserved by the others in jeopardy. This seems obvious but is often missed: when you say yes to being someplace you have said no to being everyplace else. When you say yes to spending time on something you are saying no to spending time on something else. When you say yes to being with someone you are saying no to being with others. You must be thoughtful and disciplined in your "yeses," ensuring they are spread out and appropriately reflect your priorities, if you are to have balance in your life.

But that is not all. Risk and reward, patience and urgency, listening and speaking, research and action, work and play, faith and reason, justice and mercy—every day you must seek to find and maintain balance in a myriad of aspects of life. Remember that, "There is a time for everything, and a season for every activity under heaven." That this need for balance cannot be resolved, but must be perpetually pursued, is at odds with the basic desire to get things done and forget about them—this one is a life-long quest.

CHAPTER TWENTY-EIGHT

Romeo and Juliet would be alive...

Good communication is at once critical and uncommon—and its absence drives much human hardship. Whether it is declining to ask for help when you need it, not listening well to the words and meaning of the speaker, failing to "say what you mean and mean what you say" or neglecting to "speak not so that you can be understood, but so that you cannot be misunderstood" (two of my father's favorite sayings), or a myriad of other failings, poor communication results in unnecessary confusion and misunderstanding.

Much of fiction—in books, in movies, on TV—however, depends on poor communication. Romeo and Juliet, for instance, would be alive if only the friar's message had been received. I often find myself yelling at the TV "tell her what you know", pointing out that the story would be over with everyone happy if only he did. People wander streets lost while walking past strangers who could help, move forward with errant assumptions that could be corrected with simple questions, and otherwise live in ignorance, when gaining knowledge requires simply reaching out. People with important knowledge are left frustrated when they are unable to communicate that knowledge clearly and convincingly so that it might benefit themselves and others—you may remember the myth of Cassandra, who was given the gift of knowing the future, but the curse that no one would ever believe her.

People sometimes fail to speak up when they know they should, with significant costs to themselves and others. Remember Lincoln's words, "To sin by silence when they should speak makes cowards of men". And those of Edmund Burke, "All that is necessary for evil to triumph is for good men to remain silent."

Communication, of course, has two components: the sending and the receiving. How often has each of us said, "But I told you..."? Throwing a ball at someone when they are not ready probably won't result in a successful pass. As the sender, it is your responsibility to ensure that you have the receiver's attention, that the receiver has the capacity to catch what you are throwing, and that you throw a catchable ball. As the receiver, it is your responsibility to focus on the sender, communicate your capacity to receive it, and endeavor mightily to make the catch to complete the pass—even if it is unclear or off-target. And then there are issues of attitude and tone, which can undermine either party's desire to complete the pass. Only by acting as a team, determinedly working to respect and understand each other, will you reliably communicate clearly.

One last thing: surveys of businesses perpetually indicate that poor communication—both oral and written—is the number one reason for employees being fired or on probation. Good communication is critical to your professional success as well as in your personal life.

CHAPTER TWENTY-NINE

Likes dissolve likes

Taken from chemistry, that phrase means that substances are best dissolved by solvents most similar to themselves. That is useful to know when cleaning up a mess—gasoline is best at cleaning up a greasy mess, while water is better with salt. Soap and shampoo bridge the gap between the two, being more like gasoline in structure (and the ability to clean up grease), but able to dissolve in water (which gasoline and other such solvents generally will not do— think of "oil and water").

These concepts are valuable to consider when dealing with people. Research indicates that people tend to read and best remember news from sources that share their perspectives. This may be because information from such sources simply "fits" better into your mental picture of the world (meaning the new information has "a place to go" in the organization of your brain). Or it may be that you are simply more likely to accept information from sources with which you agree (a question of open-mindedness). Or it may be that these two are really the same, related to your willingness to do the work of learning. In any case, it has strong implications for your ability to communicate well with others—and is a warning.

Regarding communication, this means you must be able to present ideas in ways that resonate with a wide range of perspectives if you are to be generally persuasive and relevant—or even listened to. That is, somehow you need to find a way to act as soap, being able to present ideas that all people understand to be related to their own. Recent research indicates that humor can be valuable in that regard, somehow breaking barriers and opening minds to learning, but you will need more than that—you need to listen and seek to understand the concerns and perspectives of others if you are to successfully communicate with them.

The warning in all of this is that you have this same tendency and need to be aware of it at all times. You may naturally relax, begin shaking your head yes, and open your mind to learning when presented with facts, ideas, and arguments that resonate with you. You need to consciously practice critical thinking and analysis when you realize that is happening, applying the same rigor you might automatically if you disagreed. You may naturally bristle or "turn off" when hearing things at odds with your view of the world or any part thereof. You need to actually seek out such perspectives, and intentionally consider each fact and idea as potentially true.

In my experience, there is something to be learned from everyone you meet and everything you hear or see— and what is shared by those with whom you initially disagree may be critically important to your developing understanding of the world and yourself. And, related to the issue of communication, people are more likely to be open to hearing your ideas if they see you are open to hearing theirs. Even if you end up "agreeing to disagree," you will develop mutual respect from such exchanges, which will contribute to the building of community and a better world.

I end with a favorite quote from John Wooden, which captures our tendency to affirm the familiar and reject the foreign:

Stubbornness we deprecate, firmness we condone
The former is our neighbor's trait, the latter is our own

CHAPTER THIRTY

The value of diversity

There is a standard exercise in management classes to demonstrate the value of working with others. Students are asked to answer a set of questions on their own and then asked to answer the same questions in groups. The groups always do better than any single individual. The conclusion of this exercise is something we all know: two (or more) heads are better than one.

But implied in this conclusion is the assumption that the various heads in the group have different ideas. If you put together people with the same background, the same education, the same culture, or from the same neighborhood, you might, in the extreme, not get any additional ideas by adding more heads (though probably you would, even in this case). If, on the other hand, you pulled people together from different cultures, races, ethnic groups, countries, etc., you would expect to get a very wide range of ideas and knowledge. It would even be reasonable to expect that a group of the "smartest" people from any one place/culture/race, etc. would not come up with answers as good as those of a same sized group composed of randomly chosen (not necessarily the "smartest") with greater diversity.

The value of diversification is seen in many areas of life. In finance, for instance, it is well understood that the "best" portfolio (the portfolio that offers the best return for a given level of risk) is not made up of the 30 "best" stocks (again, those that offer the best return for risk when considered individually). What matters is the performance of the total portfolio, which depends on both the individual performance of each stock, but also the extent to which they do not behave similarly—the lack of correlation in their returns.

The best basketball team may not be made of the five best players, but of players whose strengths and weaknesses offset and complement each other.

And consider alloys. Steel, which is composed of iron and carbon, is stronger than pure iron because carbon atoms can fit in places and create bonds that iron cannot do with itself.

More simply, no carpenter has a tool box filled with only one kind of tool: 20 hammers do not meet the range of needs that 20 varied tools would.

And yet diversity has developed a bad name with many people for two reasons. First, as you may have already experienced, our valuing of diversity has often been translated into a simple "head counting" of various populations, resulting in "reverse" discrimination (discrimination against over-represented populations). This is a fine line. It is true that a candidate's diverse perspective is of value and should be included in the overall decision. But seeking to fulfill headcount quotas without respect for overall qualification can place "beneficiaries" into situations for which they may not be prepared to be successful. Each of us deserves to be valued for the gifts we really have instead of those someone wishes we had so he can fill a quota. It seems much better to commit to using education to prepare underrepresented populations for success as the strategy for access, inclusion, and equity. Unfortunately, education is widely disparate in this country, and tends to perpetuate, instead of offset, inequity. That must be fixed. Until that is done, there is an understandable desire to promote "fairness" by other means, but that causes its own problems.

Second, despite the case for diversity made above, there are some kinds of diversity we wish were not present in our society. Few would argue, for instance, that we benefit by having representative presence of bullies or chronically dishonest people. The problem is that articulating such a list can be socially dangerous. It is obviously true that each of us might create a different list, and that some lists might include inappropriate discrimination based on unjust biases. Racism and sexism, for instance, persist in all directions. The question is whether that fact means it is not possible to identify a *just* list based on universal truths. Even people who would argue against such a list and against the existence of universal truths generally have things they "know" are wrong. Without open and honest discussion we are left with confusion and name-calling.

Despite these two issues, we must not lose sight of the essential role of diversity in our national character and success—and its value to each one of us. We are all immigrants to this land—even the "native" Americans migrated here through Siberia and Alaska.

Many of us have been resented when we first arrived, but each has eventually contributed new strength, making sacrifices for a better future and contributing diverse talents to this great alloy which is America. While most nations are built on a common heritage, culture or ethnicity, America is uncommon—perhaps even unique—in being built instead on ideas. Thus our capacity to embrace all peoples and benefit from their varied gifts.

For all of our challenges, we of this nation have learned to love our neighbors, including people unlike ourselves, to an astonishing and unprecedented degree—and that is one of our greatest strengths. We will be diminished to the extent we forget that.

CHAPTER THIRTY-ONE

Manage risk, don't avoid it

Sometimes people take risk wildly, seeming to actually wish to lose the thing being risked. Other times people seem so risk averse that they would have a very hard time accepting risk even if they realized that their very lives might depend on it. The most beneficial stance is to try to be neither risk seeking nor risk fearing, but instead try to balance and manage your risk-taking.

In the field of finance it is proposed that risk and reward should be thought of as related: that, in general, the reward you get for taking no risk is very low, and that only by taking and managing some risk will you be able to earn a higher reward. As I have often told my students, the good news about placing your retirement savings in the lowest risk investments is that your return is nearly guaranteed; the bad news about that strategy is that you will likely never retire, since the return you earn will not allow your savings to grow to the amount you need to live on. You will have certainty, but certainty of something that is not what you want. Only by accepting and managing some risk can you meet your goal. This conclusion can be translated into much of life.

But we don't always tend toward a rational response to risk.

The first problem is that we don't always accurately understand the risks to which we are exposed. I used to have a picture hanging in my office (a bank advertisement torn from a newspaper) of a man standing fishing on the edge of what looked like an island. As you looked more closely, you could see that what looked like foliage on the island was really a fin, and he was actually standing on a giant fish—with his bait dangling in front of the monster's mouth! The caption read something like, "Risk: It's not always where you expect it to be." That is true. The world is full of risk, and that is part of life. It is so easy to work at avoiding one risk, but leave ourselves exposed to another that may be less obvious but even more consequential: We once had a babysitter who responded to being scared by turning on every light in the house, but neglected to check the doors, most of which were unlocked.

The second problem is that we don't always consistently execute our strategy toward risk, even if it is a good one. Our natural tendency to accept or avoid a particular risk may make it hard to execute a strategy: An innate fear of heights might prevent us from crossing a high bridge we know is safe, exposing us to the loss of whatever is on the other side of the bridge. It is also possible that an unexpected diversion may momentarily cause us to fail to execute our strategy at a key point. One of the things I love about Saturdays in the summer is that my youngest son and I ride bikes into town for breakfast. It's a two mile ride, some of which is along a major road with a small bike lane, beside which cars are going 45 miles per hour. He and I both recognize the risk in this section and are careful to stay out of traffic. Still, it is shocking how strong the tendency is to swerve around a stick or a bump even though swerving puts us out of the bike lane and into the car lane.

Sometimes execution of our risk strategy may simply take courage that fails us when we need it.

Whatever the reason, we often end up managing risk in a way that is inconsistent with our plan—and the results can be tragic. Indeed, famed playwright Arthur Miller defined tragedy not as when someone walks under a falling piano, but when that person knows the piano is falling and walks under it anyway.

A critical part of mature risk-taking is the ability to accept the consequences of risk when they occur—which they will, even when risk is taken responsibly. Doing something that has an 80% chance of success may be your best option, but 20% of the time it will suffer failure. Accept that. Learn from it. Never second-guess it. So often I see people or groups discuss and accept a risk, but then complain and recriminate each other if things go badly. As a leader, you will never foster an entrepreneurial team if it is known you do not accept the periodic failure that comes with risk-taking.

Overall, you need to be intentional and rational about the way you manage risk. Seek to understand risk accurately; honestly assess your capacity for accepting various risks and their consequences (how would you handle the worst case scenarios?). Seek to understand the rewards or potential benefits associated with taking each kind of risk. Fashion a decision and exposure relative to each risk—and to the total risk package—that reflects your tolerance for risk balanced by the value of each reward to you. Manage each risk exposure over time—if the risk changes, it is possible your exposure should too.

I end with two favorite quotes regarding the importance of taking risk. The first hung on the wall beside my father's desk throughout my childhood and the second is an excerpt from a beloved poem:

> *Far better it is to dare mighty things, to win glorious triumphs, even though checkered by failure, than to take rank with those poor spirits who neither enjoy much nor suffer much, because they live in the gray twilight that knows not victory nor defeat.*
>
> Theodore Roosevelt

> *How dull it is to pause, to make an end,*
> *To rust unburnished, not to shine in use!*
> *As though to breathe were life.*
>
> Alfred, Lord Tennyson, *Ulysses*

CHAPTER THIRTY-TWO

Learning from jigsaw puzzles

You will often be in situations that seem overwhelming, either because there are so many problems needing solutions that you don't know where to start, or because you feel like you have no idea how to solve some of the problems. In some cases, the order in which you solve the problems is dictated by the availability of external resources needed for their solution. In others there may be urgent external need for parts of the solution that drive the order in which you must solve the component problems. Finally, it is sometimes true that solutions to some of the component problems will depend on having already resolved other component problems, which will drive the order in which you must solve the problems.

But if the above ordering issues are absent—or if it is unclear they are present—a good strategy is to start by solving the easy problems first. People sometimes refer to this as, "Going after the low-hanging fruit" (as opposed to struggling to get the fruit at the top of the tree when there is easy picking right in front of you.)

By doing so, you will often find that the hard things get easier as you go—either because you are more practiced, or because resolving the easy things makes the hard things closer to resolution. Putting together a jigsaw puzzle is a great simple example of this. A large puzzle may seem overwhelming at first, but if you begin by getting all of the border pieces together and sorting them by color, you will usually have a bunch of small puzzles that will be easier to work on. Success on these will give you clusters around which you can begin to build and begin forming the over-all solution.

This strategy of searching for something you understand as a starting point is important to remember in a wide range of circumstances. It is easy to get discouraged and give up, or suffer unnecessary hardship, because you try to "start at the beginning" or some other obvious starting point when there is no requirement to do so.

I was reminded of the strategy recently, when helping a friend cut up a large tree that had fallen in a storm. Well aware of the weight of each branch I was cutting, as well as the fact that the branches on which the fallen tree now rested were significantly bowed, I understood that the cutting of each branch was a dangerous—potentially deadly—undertaking. Indeed, our next door neighbor, who sells insurance, calls such projects "widow makers." I committed to cutting only branches that I thought I could cut safely. To the extent I could, I worked from the end of each branch, ensuring that the piece I was cutting off was as light as possible. Working in this way, I was able to remove all of the branches not touching the ground. In doing so, I had removed a great deal of weight from the bowed branches, some of which now no longer even touched the ground, and were thus easily cut. In the end, we were able

to cut up the entire tree, which I never would have imag-
ined—or thought I would have been willing to risk—when
I first saw it.

It's a simple idea, but will serve you well if you remember it: start with what you *can* do—start with the border
pieces of the puzzle—and the rest may fall into place.

CHAPTER THIRTY-THREE

Hurry to the ball, but take your time on the shot

My father used to love playing golf. When we kids first began playing with him, he spent much of the time instructing us on golf etiquette, leaving resolution of our errant shots to our experimentation and later lessons. Among the most emphasized points was the timing of play: moving along at an acceptable pace so as not to disrupt the play of other golfers. When we were young, this was a significant challenge to us, leading to a great deal of hurrying in our shots, running to find the balls, and taking our next shots—it really was a little frantic, and did not improve the quality of our shots or scores. After a little while, my father suggested we change our allocation of time, slowing down to take the shots, which were the point of the exercise, but hurrying between shots, since that part had nothing to do with our score or the point of the game. As I got older, I generalized the lesson: minimize time spent on things that don't matter so that you have more time for things that do.

There is another way of making that point, popularized by the late Stephen Covey: *Put your big rocks in first* (featured in a great video on YouTube). The idea is that you need to make sure your get the important things (the big rocks) in your life (the bucket) first, and then allow the lower priorities (smaller rocks) to fill in the space around the big rocks—otherwise, you will have a life full of low priorities with no time for the most important things. The point is that you cannot just say yes to everything and fill your time with requests as they come in—there is no reason to think the important things will come in first or most often, and if you don't dedicate time and space for them, you may never do them.

I will conclude by repeating something painfully obvious, but often forgotten: whatever you are doing, you are not doing lots of other things; whatever you are spending your money on, you are not spending it on other things; whoever you are spending time with, you are not spending time with others; when you say yes to anything you are saying no to lots of others. It is easy to get wrapped up in perfectionism, competition, or other motivations for spending resources that do not reflect your priorities. Try to be intentional about avoiding that. It is easy to think of resources (including time) as infinite when you are spending them, but they are not. Spend them wisely.

CHAPTER THIRTY-FOUR

Finding Easter Eggs

One Easter morning when I was about 5 years old, I was looking for my Easter nests. They didn't have the plastic eggs in those days and so the candy was hidden in little nests made of decorative Easter grass (which was paper, not plastic as it is now.) Each kid was given a certain space in which to search, in which there were hidden five or six nests, each about five to six inches across and filled with candy. This particular morning, my space was the kitchen. I found some of my nests pretty quickly, but then was stuck. I knew if I didn't find my last nest soon, I would have to stop searching and get ready for church, deferring my search until after breakfast and church. I didn't want that to happen.

After a little while, my mom, sensing my frustration, suggested I drop the search for a few minutes and help her get ready for breakfast by getting the orange juice out of the refrigerator. I absent-mindedly agreed. As I opened the refrigerator door, my mind still thinking of where my nest could be, my eyes landed on it, sitting on the egg carton in the refrigerator. I was young and (incorrectly) did not imagine my mother had any foresight in sending me there, but instead (never-the-less correctly) concluded that when stuck on a problem it is sometimes better to move to something else for a while, even to spend time helping someone else with his or her problem. Doing so relaxes and opens your mind—and sometimes the solution appears when you least expect it! I have used this strategy and had that happen many times in my life.

CHAPTER THIRTY-FIVE

Writing is like throwing up

I spoke in the preface about the importance of recording ideas as they hit you so that you could save those "bolts of lightning" for later use. That later use is hard work—at least it is for me. When I know I need to write something— a speech, a letter, an essay, this book—I think about what I need to say for some time, researching ideas as they occur to me, which usually leads to more ideas. I record and collect those ideas someplace so that I begin to build a "pile" of raw material, which will become the content of the written work. As I get sufficient material accumulated (often also, when I get close to the due date for the work if there is one!), I begin to review all of these ideas and try to arrange them into a coherent order and outline. As I do, I look for ways to make a continuous, cohesive, consistent, and compelling case or story out of the assortment of ideas. Usually I have an idea what that case or story is before it emerges from this process, but details often surprise me as they emerge (thus the old saying "I never knew what I thought until I wrote it down") and occasionally, the conclusion itself is different than I initially expected.

In any case, at this point, I seek to digest the entire outline and all of the ideas so that they are rolling around in my head as I walk, drive, sleep, shower—live. As a portion of the story crystalizes, I draft the paragraphs or sections that tell that part of the story—not necessarily starting at the beginning, but starting with sections as they crystallize. Little by little, I assemble more and more of the pieces of the story, trying to rearrange them as they emerge, to most clearly and compellingly tell the overall story. For me, writing on a computer is critical—both because I can type much faster than I can write (also, I can read it later when I type, but not so much when I write!), and because it allows me to easily rearrange the ordering of ideas to see which arrangement seems to work best.

Writing—the most thoughtful form of communication, the importance of which I spoke earlier—is really, really important and I want to share some ideas on process—and give you some advice and encouragement.

First some advice. I have read that "writer's block" is a result of trying to do too much at once—trying to compose, edit and refine (create a finished product) all at the same time. The process described above is my strategy for working through the process in stages. The critical thing in the early stage of writing something is that you let the ideas flow out without trying to manage them—just as in the "brainstorming" stage of problem solving, you list out possible solutions without discussion or editing. Some of your teachers may have asked you to do 5-minute "quick writes"—short bursts of writing aimed at nothing more than getting something on that page (including, perhaps, the words, "I don't know what to write…") with the hope it would teach you how to get the flow going. There is a great scene in the movie *Finding Forrester*, in which the accomplished writer tells his mentee to start retyping something the mentor had written and then, "take off with your own words once they occur to you." For myself, I have discovered that ideas often flow best when I write in the middle of the night, when, I suspect, I am too tired to overthink things.

Whatever strategy you use to get going, you need to know that writing is hard work and takes discipline—for everyone, I believe. I have read personal accounts of a wide range of writers, including Mark Twain, Ray Bradbury, and Danielle Steele, among others, attesting that the important thing is that you "get your butt in the chair" every day. Writing *something*, even when you do not feel it is inspired, is critical if you are to sustain progress and complete a project—and often that "uninspired" section turns out better than you thought, upon later reading. And editing and refining are hard—forcing myself to think through the logic for consistency and continuity is tough mental work, and rereading to polish and improve takes stamina and is grueling. I can well understand why Friedrich Nietzsche wrote, "Of all that is written, I love only what a person hath written with his blood."

For me, writing is like throwing up. I am constantly consuming information and ideas, digesting and synthesizing them until I can no longer hold them in, forcing the painful projection of thinking onto the page. Getting the ideas out and formed into a finished piece is hard work. But they were ideas churning around inside of me that had to get out. And I feel so much better once the piece is completed!

CHAPTER THIRTY-SIX

Stocks and Flows, Pools and Rivers

A swimming pool is a fixed resource that is depleted as you remove water, while a river is continually being replenished, allowing ongoing withdrawals indefinitely. Spending of savings is draining a stockpile of a limited resource and will end when the savings account is depleted, while spending out of earnings can be sustained as long as the earnings are maintained. One is stagnant; one is flowing. The extent of one is fixed and determined by its size, while the extent of the other depends on its rate of flow. And yet they are both sources of resource and they are often used interchangeably, without respect for their essential difference.

There can be a tendency, for instance, to take a one-time windfall (*a stock*), such as an inheritance check or proceeds from a sale, and use it to make the first of many payments on an ongoing expense (*a flow*), such as a new rental or salaries for new employees. Sometimes a one-time windfall is used to pay a one-time cost (thus matching a stock resource to a stock expenditure, which is appropriate), such as the outright purchase of a car, while overlooking the fact that the object of that cost, the purchased car for instance, brings with it associated ongoing expenses (flows), such as insurance, gasoline, and upkeep.

It is critical to realize whether each expense is one-time or ongoing to understand the extent of the spending commitment. Consider government spending. Keynesian theory suggests that when private sector demand (purchasing by households and businesses) drops off, the government might soften or eliminate an economic recession by temporarily spending more to offset that drop in private sector spending. The theory dictates that this increase in government spending should be on projects that can be started quickly (injecting demand quickly) and completed in months or a few years—it should be short-term (stock) spending. This ensures that government spending does not rise permanently, but only as a temporary smoothing of economy-wide demand. There is a great temptation, however, to use the opportunity of spending justified by the goal of economic recovery to implement programs that will continue generating expenses long after the recession has ended, thus permanently contributing to an ongoing deficit.

Our natural resources are perhaps the most critical area in which the concepts of stocks vs. flows (often referred to as non-renewable vs. renewable) must be considered. Fresh water coming from rain is an ongoing (if not always reliable) flow, while runoff from melting glaciers is depletion of a stock, unless the glaciers are being built up again as part of a (usually annual) cycle. This is critical to realize, since dependency on a flow source can be ongoing, but dependency on a stock source that is being depleted will eventually result in an abrupt ending. We identify renewable resources (flows) as compared to non-renewable resources (stocks), but it can be easy to drift into thinking of non-renewable resources as flows if their extent seems vast and unable to be depleted. No matter their size, stock resources will eventually be depleted if continually used. When using such resources, we are depriving future generations of access to them.

CHAPTER THIRTY-SEVEN

Kindling will not keep you warm for long; Logs cannot be lit directly

One of my strongest memories of camping with my children, whether in our back yard or somewhere else, is of my middle daughter waking up early to help get the fire started. Not necessarily an early riser on other occasions, she would pop out of her sleeping bag as soon as she heard someone rustling, wanting to be there to watch and help the precariously flickering flame grow into the fire on which we would cook our breakfast. Rain or snow or sweltering heat, she always seemed up for camping, if only for the magic of this ritual.

The dynamics of building a fire have always fascinated me too. As easy as it sometimes seems for fires to start where they are not wanted, any novice trying to get one going can testify to the challenge—and the triumph—of achieving a roaring blaze.

The object, of course, is to get the big logs going so that they warm and light the room or campsite. The challenge of getting to that state involves understanding the combined roles of air flow, fuel, and heat, as well as having the patience to begin small and build slowly. It is the latter on which I want to focus here.

You will find that many things in life must be done in stages. The end result (the blazing logs) may be your goal, but you may never get there without respecting the preconditions to achieving that goal (the lighting of kindling)—and the relationship between the two. Learning the alphabet before trying to read; learning to add before trying to understand multiplication; practicing to prepare for the game; building a small group of believers in an idea or cause as the base from which a movement grows; acting locally to achieve something globally. All include building capacity of the system, just as the kindling builds sufficient heat to get the logs going. All involve change. In some sense, kindling is a starting point, a precondition, a pathway, to change.

Clearly, your end goals are important: the logs do the "heavy lifting" and sustain the fire. You could not keep your fire going long with twigs and paper (rehearsing the alphabet, practicing but never playing, etc.) My point is that it is very easy to focus just on the logs (your end goals), but you will never get the logs going without giving time and attention to the kindling. Each has a strength to add; each has a weakness. The strength of each offsets the weakness of the other. It is easy to appreciate the warmth and glow of burning logs. With time, you may learn to love the crackle of kindling as much.

CHAPTER THIRTY-EIGHT

Nurse logs

Olympic National Park (in the northwest corner of the state of Washington) is an amazing place, with glacier-covered mountains on the east side of the park, and temperate rainforest on the west side (caused by the mountains catching all the rain as it comes in off the coast.) The rainforest is damp and lush, with many unusual plants and growth patterns.

One of these is the nurse log—a fallen tree that supports a wide range of animal and plant life as it decomposes into rich soil. My family discovered nurse logs during a visit to the park many years ago. The first evidence we saw of a nurse log lacked the log itself: a mighty conifer stood an hundred feet tall, resting not on the straight and solid trunk base you would expect, but on a delicate pattern of roots lifting the solid trunk base three feet off the ground. It seemed as if the massive tree was standing on its tiptoes. At first, we thought this was the normal growing pattern of some unusual species of tree—like the Cyprus knee. Further inspection revealed, however, both that there were many similar trees nearby with trunks firmly planted on the ground, and that the roots of the "tiptoe tree" seemed to form a tunnel. It was not long before we saw a nurse log at work and understood the formation of the tiptoe tree. As a fallen tree rots, it becomes an increasingly rich resting place upon which seeds land, germinate, and grow into trees. At first, their tiny roots are planted solely in the rotting log. But as the sapling grows, it reaches its roots around the log to plant a network of support in the firm soil on either side of the log. As time passes, the log dissipates into the earth and the sapling grows into a mighty tree with a foundation that tells the story of its beginning.

Many things in our world are like that, some superficial, some more important. We have embedded window "frames" between layers of our windows to mimic the style from a time when creating a window out of one large piece was more difficult and expensive than creating a large window by combining smaller pieces of glass in panes. Fried rice and French toast—in fact toast itself—were once strategies for dealing with stale leftovers, but are now favorites on their own. Like these, the persistence of many solutions past the points at which they are needed is innocuous, costless, and often quaint and nostalgic.

There is an old story that falls into that category. A husband and wife were once hosting a family reunion for which they were cooking a large roast. Before putting it in the oven, the wife cut the end off the roast and placed the additional piece alongside the roast in the pan. This seeming peculiar to him, the husband asked why she did that, to which his wife replied, "That is how you cook a roast." When he asked for further information, she simply said, "That is how my mother always did it." With his mother-in-law in the other room, he decided to take the opportunity to find out more, but when he asked her, she too replied, "That is how my mother always did it." As luck would have it, his wife's maternal grandmother was also at the party, so the husband persisted, seeking to unravel the mystery. When asked the question, the matriarch laughed out loud and said, "I used to have a very small oven and had to cut the end off the roast so it would fit in the oven!"

You will not believe how often we "cut the end off the roast" just because "that's the way it's done"—even when we are the ones who established the adaptation for the "small oven" in the first place! Habits are so easy to form and we so often go through motions without realizing we don't need to do it that way anymore. And often it doesn't matter.

But there are other vestiges that impede progress and success if left unexamined and unmodified. As discussed earlier, self-images developed during childhood in relation to family relationships often persist well after adults have left the family environments that formed them. Teams or businesses will sometimes design a role around the capabilities or tendencies of a specific person filling that role, which may impose problems if his or her successors are expected to fill the customized role as it was designed for their predecessor. Likewise, processes and policies established in response to specific circumstances need to be reviewed and rewritten when those circumstances change—or you may be left responding to something that is no longer true. I cannot tell you how often we keep doing the same thing without thinking—and telling others they have to do it that way when there is no reason they should. As my father used to say, "Doing what has always been done is a dangerous substitute for thinking."

Which brings me to another story…

When I was growing up in the 1960's, high jumpers used to land on two- to four-inch stuffed mats. Sometimes a few of these mats were piled up, but they really did not soften the landing much, and everyone jumping—from elementary school kids to Olympic champions—had to land in a way that ensured they would be able to walk away uninjured. There were two jumping styles: the scissors, which allowed you to land on your feet, and the straddle roll, which allowed you to land on your feet or side—either way you would be assured of a safe landing and the ability to jump again. And then, in the mid-sixties, someone invented the 3 foot tall, air-filled cushions you see today, which completely changed the landing experience—now you needed to tell the jumpers to get up because they were prone to want to relax or bounce around in the cushion after jumping. And yet, everyone continued to jump by doing the scissors or the roll. Only one person, a guy named Dick Fosbury, realized that the new cushion meant more than comfort—it meant that he could now land just about any way he wanted to and still live to tell the tale. Only Dick Fosbury was able to let go of his preconceived notions about how to jump and consider how he would design a jump now, given the new realities of his sport. Fosbury entered the 1968 Olympics doing the impossibly awkward- looking "Fosbury Flop," with which he proceeded to win the gold medal and set a new Olympic record— and now everyone jumps that way.

You can learn a great deal from Dick Fosbury. The world is changing all around you constantly. Every day, every time you do anything of importance you need to ask yourself, "Given new developments, is this the way I would do it if I were designing the process from scratch to take best advantage of current knowledge and resources?" Doing so may get you into trouble some times (you need to think through innovations and explore them carefully to make sure you don't "break your neck"—or anyone else's), but it will definitely keep your life interesting, and will allow you to add value wherever you are.

CHAPTER THIRTY-NINE

Sex is like Super Glue

Parents and others may tell you to avoid sexual relations except within the marriage relationship. I don't need to tell you that this is widely ignored and even considered unnecessary or impossible by many in our culture. What I do want to share is the pervasiveness and seriousness of the consequences of ignoring that advice. You already know about STDs and pregnancy. I want to focus on the consequences for relationships, which seem much more profound and permanent.

Sex early in a relationship causes premature bonding, often resulting in permanence to relationships that are not the right fit. Indeed, recent research on brain chemistry has revealed that two chemicals, Oxytocin and Vasopressin, are released in the brain during and after sex, and that each creates psychological binding between the individuals involved—your body actually creates "love potions" that draw you closer and raises your commitment to your partner.

Think of superglue applied to pieces that don't really fit together—they will get stuck together, but the bond will not be as strong as if the pieces actually fit together in the first place and were cemented together by the glue. Though a great challenge, I really believe it is in your interest to steer clear of sex in relationships, seeking to find a mate based on qualities other than sexual attraction, which will grow in a loving relationship. Passion can be fleeting, while commitment is by nature persistent. It seems to me wiser to believe that passion will come out of your commitment than to hope commitment will come out of your passion.

Finding a good life partner and mate is one of the most important decisions of your life—it will impact your children, your spiritual development, your career, and countless other things in your life. The challenge is that you only get to make that decision once (it is hoped), and that comes before you have much life experience that would help you in the decision.

You are growing up in a particularly challenging time with respect to dating. When I was young, family structure and roles seemed better defined, and it seemed widely accepted that things like modesty and self-discipline were good (though that certainly began changing while I was growing up). My sense of current pop culture is that this is no longer true. Rarely referring to development of real relationships, the pop songs I hear seem to focus more than ever before on either seduction or lack of relationship. I believe these two are linked.

The end result of all of this for you is that there seem to have developed two cultures among the youth: those who are part of this new culture and those who reject it. For the latter, dating seems less safe than ever before—the expectation of sex can get brought into the relationship at any time. The result has been that those who reject—or fear—the new cultural "norm" have withdrawn from dating, even attending events like proms in groups—often of the same sex—if at all. Traditional forums for exploring male-female relationships have been significantly altered, leaving it to your generation to create and explore new ones.

In that regard, I know there is a lot of recent psychological research on matchmaking available now, which informs many of the sites such as Match.com and eHarmony. I don't know much about them, but would probably research them if I were in your place to help me understand factors I should consider. I also recommend Timothy Keller's book, *The Meaning of Marriage*, which describes the potential of a committed marriage as a deep friendship in which two people help each other grow in their relationships. I really think this book is valuable.

My own experience tells me that shared values are critical to a fruitful and committed marriage. Any marriage—any relationship—will go through periods of difficulty, but knowing you respect, share, and support the core values of your spouse will give you a foundation of trust, which is absolutely necessary.

In the end, you should marry someone you believe does and will challenge and empower you to be a better person in every way. At the start of a relationship, you are only seeing (perhaps through rose-colored glasses) the beginning of the trajectory your life might follow with that person (including, importantly, what your children will be like), so you must observe that trajectory as closely and as objectively as you can. As hard as it might be, you should run from a relationship in which you are drawn to things you know are not right. That is not to say that someone good for you will always make you happy—while it may be true you should "beware the kisses of enemies and value the bruises from friends", it can be hard not to enjoy the former nor sting from the latter.

Finally, I hope that, if you marry, you are lucky enough to find a lasting, loving, healthy relationship. Marriage is hard work—partly because it asks you to love a person not like you, partly because it asks you to love a person who is ever changing, and partly because it challenges you to grow into a better person. But it is worth the work and challenge. Really.

CHAPTER FORTY

Commitment

Legend tells us that as soon as Julius Caesar's conquering forces landed on Great Britain, he assembled them on the cliffs of Dover to see an amazing thing: the ships on which they had just arrived were set on fire. History records instances in which other generals have used the same strategy. All of these leaders were motivated by the same knowledge: You behave differently if you are completely committed.

Commitment means you know there is a way to make this happen and you will do what it takes. It's not "let's see how this works out" or "we'll give it a try", but, "we know there is a solution and we just need to find it."

I bring this up in the context of the previous chapter, and as related to the topic of marriage. Given statistics that, on average, half of marriages end in divorce, and the feeling of uncertainty regarding one's ability to make good on a vow to love someone "until death do us part," it is reasonable—perhaps even a position of integrity for someone taking such a vow seriously—to ask, "How can I have any confidence in my commitment to marriage?"

First, we need to recognize there is an important problem with using statistics: averages can be misleading. I have recently been treated for a serious health condition, the relapse rate for which is, on average, about 30 per cent. But it turns out that there are several factors within my control that can significantly alter my chances of relapse relative to that average. Eating lots of high fat and sugary foods may double my risk. Eating lots of broccoli and other vegetables may cut it in half. Exercising three times a week and a wide range of other behaviors may cut it significantly further. In short, I am not stuck with the 30 per cent relapse rate. I can significantly increase my chances of survival by behaving differently. And the same is true for marriage.

What, then, are some strategies that might increase the likelihood your marriage will survive (and even thrive!), thereby giving you reason for confidence in commitment? Again, Timothy Keller's wonderful book, *The Meaning of Marriage*, is full of ideas—as well as reasons the commitment of marriage is so important and valuable. I cannot recommend it too strongly to anyone considering (or in the midst of) marriage.

One important strategy was the topic of the last chapter: avoiding sex early in the relationship so that you can explore the depth of your compatibility before the "superglue" of sex binds you together prematurely.

A second strategy is related to something a wise friend once told me: all conflict is situational. While perhaps overstated, the idea is that any two people or peoples can get along well, given the right circumstances, and the same people can clash, given the wrong circumstances. You may have seen how a common enemy can unite adversaries (at least for a time), and may have heard the expression, "politics makes strange bedfellows." Even best friends fight in

certain situations. The challenge of maintaining friendships is to know the situations in which you enjoy each
other's company (so that you can frequent them) and the
situations in which you tend toward conflict (so that you
can avoid them—and if not that, at least anticipate and
manage them.)

Anyone who has ever been married (happily or not)
will tell you that the myriad of situations in which married
couples find themselves expose them to all of the above
and much, much more—especially if you are lucky enough
to have a family. Life gets crazy. Time, money and focus
will get away from you if you're not careful—and sometimes even if you are. You need to know how to find each
other in the fog—and care enough to always try. "Being in
love" is a feeling that comes and goes. Loving is a con-
scious act that transcends feelings. You need to learn to
will to love, even when you don't want to.

But how can you learn that and develop confidence
that you will always be able to love each other? By exposing
your relationship to a wide range of situations *before you are
married.* If you are smart enough to go to pre-marriage
counseling (more on that below), they will almost certainly
ask how you recover from fights. One of the worst answers
is, "We never fight"—not because disharmony is good, but
because it is inevitable in the messiness of living together.
You need to give your relationship time to experience a
wide range of situations, good and bad. As you do, your
confidence will grow that you can "weather any storm" and
are capable of making the commitment to marriage.

A third strategy is to learn from the experience of others. Think of older couples whose marriages you admire
and ask them to share their secrets. Pre-marriage counseling is available in most churches and many other places.

Participate in such sessions in one or more institutions—*but be careful to choose institutions you believe reflect your values or the counseling they give you may not.*

Employing these strategies can give you confidence that you are ready to make—and make good on—the commitment to love someone for a lifetime.

Epilogue

Twenty years ago, I read an article written by the president of one of the big video game manufacturers talking about the educational value of video games. He detailed how the games are designed so that new challenges and capabilities are introduced sequentially, building on top of each other, so that every challenge teaches you things you will need to know for the next challenge. His goal was to convince parents that video games were great learning experiences and that they should allow their children to play them often. Indeed, that argument is still made, and not only by those working at video game makers: just recently, at an academic conference I attended, one of the presenters suggested that well-written collaborative video games may be the most powerful problem-solving and teamwork-developing learning experiences available to any of us.

I've often thought of all of this as I've watched my children playing educational video and computer games. Their purpose of design and motivational power is stunning. Most recently, observing my youngest daughter and her friends unravel Nancy Drew computer-based mysteries has reinforced my admiration of these exercises. Listening as she and her accomplices pool knowledge to solve puzzles, decipher codes, answer historical, geographical, or other factual questions, choose the person with the best small-motor skills to complete a required task, and otherwise work collaboratively to solve problems, all while maintaining the "executive function" of retaining focus on the ultimate problem to be solved, is compelling evidence of the thoughtfulness and success of the design.

It is often said that great writing contains no paragraph, no sentence, no word that is not needed to accomplish its goal. In good literature—and even in sitcoms such as "Seinfeld"—the stories of all characters are woven together, with the actions and needs of each filling in holes in the stories of, and meeting the needs of, others. A Shakespeare play can seem impossibly disorganized, with so many characters having so many seemingly unsolvable problems right up until the last five minutes when, suddenly, it becomes obvious that all of their problems solve each other, all is resolved, and everyone lives happily ever after (unless, as one of my children pointed out, it is a tragedy).

If there is such purpose of design in the work of human authors, it seems easy to believe that there is also purpose in the design of your life. As I've tried to describe in a myriad of ways throughout this book, it seems to me that there is significant evidence all around us to support such belief. On a day-to-day basis this can give you the capacity for peace in the midst of adversity, and confidence that, no matter what happens, things will be okay.

This book began with a poem by Rudyard Kipling. I want to end with one from Mother Teresa:

People are often unreasonable, illogical and self-centred;
  Forgive them anyway
If you are kind, people may accuse you of selfish, ulterior motives;
  Be kind anyway
If you are successful, you will win some false friends and some true enemies;
  Succeed anyway
People may cheat you;
  Be honest and frank anyway
What you spend years building, someone could destroy overnight;
  Build anyway
If you find serenity and happiness, they may be jealous;
  Be happy anyway
The good you do today, people will often forget tomorrow;
  Do good anyway
Give the world the best you have, and it may never be enough;
  Give the world the best you've got anyway
  You see, in the final analysis, it is between you and God;
  It is never between you and them anyway.

—Mother Teresa

Wood for the fire: Suggested further readings

Some Christian writers (and their writings) I have found useful include:

- C.S. Lewis (*Mere Christianity* and *The Screwtape Letters*, among others),
- Thomas Merton (*The Seven Story Mountain*),
- Soren Kierkegaard (*Purity of the Heart is to Will One Thing, Works of Love, Philosophical Fragments, Practice in Christianity*, and many others),
- Blaise Pascal (*Pensées*),
- Tolstoy (*A Confession*),
- Martin Luther King, Jr. (*Strength to Love*)
- Hans Kuhn (*On Being a Christian*),
- Francis Collins(*The Language of God: A Scientist Presents Evidence for Belief*),
- St. Thomas Aquinas (*Summa Theologica*, among others),
- Pope John Paul II (*Fides et Ratio*),
- Mother Teresa (*A Simple Path*, among others)

- Lee Strobel (a series of "The Case For" books),
- Justo Gonzalez (*Santa Biblia*),
- Ravi Zachariah (*Beyond Opinion, Why Jesus?* and others)
- Catherine Marshall (*A Man Called Peter, John Doe, Disciple*, and others),
- Shane Claiborne (*The Irresistible Revolution*) and
- Timothy Keller(*The Reason for God, The Prodigal God*, and others).

Some prominent atheist (and their writings) who actively oppose belief in God, arguing that such belief results in a wide range of ills include:

- Richard Dawkins (*The God Delusion*), and
- Christopher Hitchens (*God Is Not Great*),

Others who study the role faith plays in people's lives, their behavior, and society, without predisposition as to its harm or good include:

- David Sloan Wilson (*Darwin's Cathedral*)
- Scott Atran (*In Gods We Trust*)

Western philosophers who have done work that is directly related to faith include:

- Thomas Hobbes (*Leviathan*),
- John Locke (*An Essay Concerning Human Understanding*, and *Letters Concerning Toleration*)
- René Descartes (*Meditations on First Philosophy*),
- Immanuel Kant (*Critique of Pure Reason*), and
- Friedrich Nietzsche (*Beyond Good and Evil*).

I have also learned from philosophers coming out of Muslim, Hindu, Buddhist, and other faith traditions, who have challenged me to develop and sharpen my thinking. Two popular and valuable examples are,

- *Te-Tao Ching*, by Lao Tse, and
- *The Prophet*, by Kalil Gibran.

Three centuries of historical analysis and criticism of the Bible and Christianity can be found represented in the works of:

- Will and Ariel Durant (*The Story of Civilization*),
- Michael Grant (*Jesus: An Historian's Review of the Gospels*), and
- Graham Stanton (*The Gospels and Jesus*), among many others.

A wonderful history of the Middle East from the Middle Eastern perspective is provided by Tamim Ansary in *Destiny Disrupted*, while a detailed history of wars within and between Western Europe and the Middle East can be found in *Worlds at War*, by Anthony Pagden.

Writings and research on character include:

- Paul Tough, NY Times, September 14, 2011 "*What if the Secret to Success is Failure?*"
- Christopher Peterson and Martin Seligman, *Character Strengths and Virtues: A Handbook and Classification*
- Linda and Richard Eyre, *Teaching Your Children Joy, Teaching Your Children Values, and Teaching your Children Responsibility*

- H. Stephen Glenn and Jane Nelson, *Raising Self-Reliant Children in a Self-Indulgent World*

Wonderful audio resources for children are also available through Brite Music.

I have found Transactional Analysis, as described in the book *Born to Win* by Muriel James helpful in understanding issues related to identity and relationships.

Some stories of people who have realized how to find more in their lives include,

- Wendy Kopp (founder of Teach for America based on her undergraduate thesis), *One Day All Chlidren*
- Geoffrey Canada (founder of the Harlem Children's Zone), *Reaching up for Manhood*
- Muhammad Yunus (Nobel prize winner for his work on microlending), *Banker to the Poor*
- Katie Davis (founder of Amazima Ministries), *Kisses from Katie*

Each has started very small, but made a big difference. You can too.

ABOUT THE AUTHOR

Bill Clyde is a father of five, college professor and provost. He earned a PhD in economics from Edinburgh University in Scotland, a master's degree in chemistry from New York University, and a bachelor's degree in chemistry and economics from DePauw University. Bill has published in the areas of chemistry, finance, chaos theory, learning theory, and technology, traveled to 25 countries, served on the boards of several non-profit organizations, and was a currency trader for six years before returning to academe.

CPSIA information can be obtained at www.ICGtesting.com
Printed in the USA
BVOW04s1214130914

366646BV00007B/36/P